Coming Into Alignment Through Character Refinement

Pathways Into Your Prophetic Purpose

ISBN 978-0-9975864-3-5

Unless otherwise stated, all Scripture quotations are taken from the King James Version (KJV) of the Bible.

~Dedication~

This book is dedicated to all the Rabbis and Torah Teachers who taught us Torah. My prayer of dedication is that they will know Yeshua Ha Mashiach who caused me to fall in love with His Torah.

TABLE OF CONTENTS

Introduction ……………………………………………………….7

Chapter 1. The Qualification for Exaltation into Destiny: Taking Responsibility – Reuben, Simeon, Levi, Judah ……..11

Chapter 2. The Selfishness Syndrome – Elimelech, Mahlon, Chilion, Orpah ………………………………………………35

Chapter 3. Chesed: The Diadem of Destiny – Ruth………….52

Chapter 4. Coming Into Perfection Through Character Correction – Joseph ………………………………………………66

Chapter 5. The Most Important Biblical Success Secret: Purity of Heart – David ………………………………………….81

Chapter 6. The Gift of Self-Scrutiny –David………………….98

Chapter 7. Downfalls to Destiny: Inconsistency in Character – Saul …………………………………………………..115

INTRODUCTION

Coming into Alignment Through Character Refinement

What is the meaning of "coming into alignment through character refinement"? It is the most important success secret of the Bible. Character traits are the very criteria for covenant. God said to Abraham, "Walk before Me and be thou perfect" (Genesis 17:1). Perfect does not mean never failing and having a flawless life without failures. Perfect in a Hebrew sense of scripture is the word "tamim" (Strong's Hebrew 8549), which means without guile, blameless, and pure of heart. It is our highest destiny to walk "blameless before God," as we see in the books of Ephesians and Philippians.

Ephesians 1:4 KJV
According as He hath chosen us in Him before the foundation of the world, that we should be holy and without blame before Him in love.

Philippians 2:15 KJV

That ye may be blameless and harmless, the sons of God, without rebuke, in the midst of a crooked and perverse nation, among whom ye shine as lights in the world.

Beloved, I have written this book for several reasons:

1. My desire is to help you understand the true nature of the tests that will determine your destiny in life. By the grace of God, this book is designed to provide instruction like a spiritual GPS that will help guide you through the dark, difficult days into the full possession of promises.

2. I want to help you achieve victory and deliverance over the strongest struggle and enemy in your life.

3. Most importantly, I want you to understand the primary importance of Biblical character development, from Genesis to Revelation. We will examine the lives of those who Scripture qualifies as worthy of the diadem of destiny because of their impeccable character traits.

Beloved, my prayer for you is that this book will help you pass every test in order to experience God's best. Throughout the Bible, we see that character traits or "middot" (plural form of "middah," Strong's Hebrew 4060), are given to us for an examination for exaltation into destiny. I want to take you on a journey to view the lives of individuals who experienced challenge, victory, trauma, and sometimes even weakness and dysfunction, and used their pain to train for greatness. What makes this so exciting is that each one of us can truly relate to some of the situations that these individuals experienced like rejection, being misunderstood, or disposition issues like mood swings that some of the most chosen individuals of the bible confronted and conquered.

Every individual selected and elected in scripture for greatness had one special character trait that they developed and brought to the highest pinnacle of perfection. For Abraham, it was chesed, or God's love in action. For David, it was tamim, or purity of heart. For Esther, it was humility. For Ruth, it was selfless chesed. For you, there is one special character trait ("middah" in Hebrew) that, if you find it and develop it, shall lead you into the path of promise, destiny, and breakthrough.

Seeking Your Success,
Dr. Michelle Corral +

CHAPTER ONE

The Qualification for Exaltation into Destiny

Taking Responsibility
-Reuben, Simeon, Levi, Judah-

Have you ever wondered why certain people were chosen for great things and why others seemed to not seize the opportunities for greatness? Is leadership and destiny something given only to those privileged individuals fortunate enough to have talent, pedigree, intelligence, beauty, education, status, and wealth? What is the difference between being "called" and "chosen"?

In Hebrew, the concept of being "chosen" is based on character traits that have been proven and worthy of leadership. In Hebrew, the word "chosen" is "bachir" (Strong's Hebrew 972). The secret of being "bachir" or "chosen" is one of the primary prophetic objectives given to us by Moses in the book of Genesis.

In the book of Genesis, we have unusual irregularities throughout the text. How is it that all the firstborn are not really the "firstborn"? The Bible tells us about several individuals who were firstborn in birth order, but not by the standards of truly being "bachir" or "chosen." We see this unusual pattern perpetuated throughout Genesis: Jacob is chosen over Esau, Joseph is chosen over Reuben, and Ephraim is chosen over Manasseh. It seems a tad complicated, but it's very simple. The firstborn who had the calling did not meet the requirement of being "bachir" or "chosen."

THE FOUR SONS OF JACOB

Exodus 1 very blatantly, in its unusual presentation of the Shevatim (tribes), highlights the fact that the firstborn are not always "bachir" or "chosen." The text unveils a downfall to a destiny that could have been achieved if there had been a character adjustment. Is it really possible to miss the miraculous call of destiny all based on refusal to recognize the need for a character adjustment?

Exodus 1:1-4 KJV

[1] Now these are the names of the children of Israel, which came into Egypt; every man and his household came with Jacob. [2] Reuben, Simeon, Levi, and Judah, [3] Issachar, Zebulun, and Benjamin, [4] Dan, and Naphtali, Gad, and Asher.

The first four are in the order of their birth with Reuben born first, Simeon second, Levi third, and Judah fourth, but the rest are out of order. One might ask why are the first four in birth order and the others all mixed up. Moses deliberately placed them that way because he had a prophetic agenda. The first four are in birth order because we are going to see something about being denied destiny. Reuben was actually the firstborn or the "bekowr" (Strong's Hebrew 1060) in his family, but the firstborn blessing passed from him on to his younger brothers to finally rest upon Judah. Even though technically the Bible tells us that the bekowr is passed on to Joseph (Genesis 49:22-26), this scripture is going to show us that the scepter is never going to depart from Judah and that Judah really was the one who received the firstborn blessing, even though he was the fourth oldest son. Reuben, Simeon, and Levi were all disqualified, but in Exodus, we will see that Levi received his position back through repentance.

Reuben

Have you ever met someone who had every advantage for dream and destiny, but never could break out of his issues? The person that I am referring to is Reuben, who had a tremendous crown and calling waiting for him, but never seized the opportunities for character correction and missed his miracle. Reuben was called to be the firstborn, but was never chosen. This is an individual who stayed stuck in his issues for his entire life. No matter what opportunities were given to him in the natural, his undealt-with personal pain became a block to the blessing of being "bachir" or "chosen." He never moved out of potential to full promise because of the lack in his character development.

Let's continue with a little more background information to better understand the situation. The Bible lists the names of all those that came into Egypt in the book of Exodus.

Exodus 1:1-5 KJV
[1] Now these are the names of the children of Israel, which came into Egypt; every man and his household came with Jacob. [2] Reuben, Simeon, Levi, and Judah, [3] Issachar, Zebulun, and Benjamin, [4] Dan, and Naphtali, Gad, and Asher. [5] And all the souls that came out of the loins of Jacob were seventy souls: for Joseph was in Egypt already.

We can see further information about those who came into Egypt in the book of Genesis.

Genesis 46:26 KJV
All the souls that came with Jacob into Egypt, which came out of his loins, besides Jacob's sons' wives, all the souls were threescore and six.

In Genesis 46, we see "souls" written seven times. The Bible is highlighting that these are the souls that originally went into Egypt with Jacob when he was going to meet Joseph for the first time after 22 years of being separated. In Exodus 5:1, the word "souls" is also included a superfluous amount of times. The text shows us that the subjugation of the children of Israel did not begin first with the physical subjugation; the subjugation of the sons of

Jacob was primarily in the soul. When we begin to understand that their captivity was in the soul, we can begin to understand the depths of the redemption that was done for the children of Israel when they left Egypt.

What does it mean to be captive in the soul in Egypt? To us Gentiles, when we read Egypt in the text, it just means Egyptians or Egypt, referring to a culture in the Middle East on the continent of Africa, and a group of people that live in Northern Africa that subjugated the children of Israel for 400 years. However, beloved, there are some concepts within the Hebrew language for which there is no English equivalent. In English, there is no word that will adequately translate the concept to our understanding. The word "Egypt" comes from the Hebrew word "Mitsrayim" (Strong's Hebrew 4714). This does not apply to a group of people in Northern Africa, but instead is a term that means limitations, a "narrow place," and a place that we cannot break out of. Another meaning is "borders," meaning something that locks us and that we cannot break past.

In Genesis 29, there is an unbearable dysfunctional emotional burden placed on Reuben that caused him to stay stuck in Mitsrayim and never get out.

Genesis 29:31-32 KJV

[31] And when the Lord saw that Leah was hated, he opened her womb: but Rachel was barren. [32] And Leah conceived, and bare a son, and she called his name Reuben: for she said, Surely the Lord hath looked upon my affliction; now therefore my husband will love me.

This text shows us Leah's personality pattern; she felt very rejected by Jacob because he loved Rachel more than her, because of the night that Laban switched the brides (Genesis 29:21-30). In reality, Jacob did not hate her, but Leah felt hated compared to the way that Jacob loved Rachel. In stating that Leah was "hated," the Bible is showing us that God always sees our feelings, and that God even validates our feelings. Leah feels that "If Jacob doesn't love me, my life is not going to be full. If Jacob doesn't love me the way that he loves my sister, then life is so bitter and life is not worth living." These things are placed in the Word of God because God wants to touch us, and Scripture wants to reach those of us who feel the same way.

Leah gives birth to her first child (Reuben) not only because she wanted a child, but also because she thinks bearing a child will make Jacob love her. Thus, the child is immediately born with a heavy burden. Reuben feels that "it is my responsibility is to make my father love my mother," because that is the word Leah spoke over his life by naming him Reuben: "Behold, a son: therefore my husband will now love me." The destiny that Leah gave to Reuben is in his name. Reuben is picking up on this dynamic between his mother and father every day and feeling overly responsible for his mother's burden; his entire life, he feels that it is his responsibility to make Jacob love Leah. Perhaps it was engrained in his mind since he was a child that he has to "fix mommy." He also incorporated the rejection that his mother felt from his father unto himself, which gave him rejection issues with Jacob.

Scripture brings all of this to light because no one is perfect. We all have some sort of dysfunction in our personality that we have developed from personal pain or from just living in this world.

MC+

The secret of character development is not being born perfect, or having the perfect home and perfect parents.

The secret of character development is not being born perfect, or having the perfect home and the perfect parents; the secret of character development in the context of the Bible is through overcoming the negative character traits that are developed from our dysfunction and personal pain. I call this "coming into perfection through character correction."

We can see there is a dysfunctional dynamic between Leah and Reuben. Reuben needs to allow his mother to just be his mother, and to not bear the burden of his mother's grief and unnecessary guilt. This dynamic causes Reuben to become a man that has no confidence as the firstborn. Reuben develops character traits where he feels entitled, and character traits that result in his constantly trying to prove that he is the firstborn using wicked methods, which we will see later in the text.

This dysfunctional dynamic of rejection felt by Reuben from his father is the source of the pain that kept him crippled most of his life. By not overcoming this personal pain, it developed a weakness that was never intended for his life. As the firstborn, the middah of his character trait would have been the excellency of strength and power (Genesis 40:39). He was ordained to be the excellency of Jacob's strength, full of the character traits of taking initiative and taking responsibility. Instead, Reuben remained stuck in the mitsrayim of the soul and never came out. At the time of the giving of the bracha or blessing in Genesis 49, Jacob pronounces the destiny and what it's going to take to possess it to Reuben, which includes overcoming his weakness of "being unstable as water." Jacob is truly giving Reuben the insight to his own weakness on his deathbed, that if he steps up to the plate as a leader and takes initiative, which means taking responsibility, there is no limit to what God will do for him. Unfortunately we never see the reality of taking the responsibility or stepping up to the plate through Reuben or his descendants. When his younger brother Joseph is sold into slavery, what does Reuben do? He leaves.

Genesis 37:23-24,29 KJV

[23] And it came to pass, when Joseph was come unto his brethren, that they stript Joseph out of his coat, his coat of many colours that was on him; [24] And they took him, and

cast him into a pit: and the pit was empty, there was no water in it... [29] And Reuben returned unto the pit; and, behold, Joseph was not in the pit; and he rent his clothes.

As the firstborn, Reuben should have taken responsibility for Joseph and told his brothers, "Over my dead body are you going to sell this boy. You are going to have to kill me first before you kill him." But Reuben does not say this; instead, he flees. Like Jacob said, he is as unstable as water. Joseph is in the pit, and Reuben leaves. Reuben does not display the leadership qualities that the Bible requires, and he has no strength. He has never perfected the character trait of gevurah (strength, discipline, taking the initiative).

When we are so obsessed with our rejection and what we have been through, we have a tendency to think about our rejection and ourselves 24/7. We may have thoughts such as "Nobody loves me, nobody respects me, nobody thinks anything of me, nobody acknowledges who I am" that

MC+

When we are so obsessed with our rejection and what we have been through, we have a tendency to think about our rejection and ourselves 24/7.

continually circulate in our minds. When a person has been hurt, abused, or lives in an isolated world of their thoughts going 24 hours a day, this becomes self-obsession that stifles the qualities of leadership from ever being developed within that person. It feeds the negative character trait of selfishness, which is the source of all sin and self-destruction. The Bible is giving us credentials for leadership, with one qualification being laying our lives down on the line and taking a risk to save somebody else.

Reuben failed on every level, despite the fact that that heaven gave Reuben every opportunity to correct his character. Reuben uses a form of masculinity that is not true masculinity to try to prove himself as the firstborn. Historically speaking, in ancient Biblical times, when the father dies, the father's concubine usually goes to the oldest son as a symbol of the son taking the place of the father as the leader in the family. After Rachel dies, Reuben takes Bilhah, the maid of Rachel and concubine of Jacob, to prove that he is the firstborn (Genesis 35:22). He does all this to prove that he is the leader of the 12 tribes and to prove that he is taking the place of Jacob in his desperate need to approve himself in his masculinity.

The methods that Reuben used to try to prove his firstborn position were in need of therapeutic dimensions of deliverance, and we see a serious failure of leadership and fallout in leadership qualities as a result. There were very strong issues within Reuben that he never confronted within himself.

In Jacob's last words to his 12 sons before he dies, when he is seeing into the future and prophesying over his sons, he says this of Reuben:

Genesis 49:3-4 KJV
[3] Reuben, thou art my firstborn, my might, and the beginning of my strength, the excellency of dignity, and the excellency of power: [4] Unstable as water, thou shalt not excel; because thou wentest up to thy father's bed; then defiledst thou it: he went up to my couch.

Because Reuben never stepped up to the plate as a leader, the firstborn birthright passed from Reuben to the second son, Simeon.

Simeon

While the birthright should have automatically passed on to Simeon, Simeon gets denied destiny as well. The Bible tells us what Jacob said about Simeon on his deathbed:

Genesis 49:5-7 KJV
[5] Simeon and Levi are brethren; instruments of cruelty are in their habitations. [6] O my soul, come not thou into their secret; unto their assembly, mine honour, be not thou united: for in their anger they slew a man, and in their selfwill they digged down a wall. [7] Cursed be their anger, for it was fierce; and their wrath, for it was cruel: I will divide them in Jacob, and scatter them in Israel.

Simeon and Levi did a very wicked thing in response to a violation of their sister Dinah. They took matters into their own hands and executed vengeance not just upon the perpetrator, but upon all the men of that city (Genesis 34). This is why Jacob says he sees the weapons of cruelty within them. Simeon and Levi both had severe anger issues, and Simeon never overcame his issues. As a result, you will never see Simeon or his seed ever accomplishing anything in all of the Bible. The tribe of Simeon has no leaders or heroes and becomes the smallest tribe. Simeon is scattered throughout all the tribes of Israel and only have a small strip of land that is technically within the borders of Judah. In fact, the blessing that Moses gives in Deuteronomy 33 is denied to the tribe of Simeon.

Levi

Levi, on the other hand, had the same pain and issues as Simeon; they were both perpetrators in the violent act in Genesis 34 and they both had anger that was out of control. Simeon never corrected or confronted his pain. But the Bible is making it very obvious that something happened to Levi; the tribe of Levi begins "shuvah" or repentance. Levi begins a lifestyle of taking accountability and correction. When Levi gets to Egypt, he realizes that "we sold Joseph into slavery, so now we are becoming slaves. God, we are responsible for all of the tribes being brought down to Egypt because of how we behaved towards our brother. So we are going to start amending our behavior."

Levi did not recover the birthright in time since it eventually rested on Judah because of his taking ownership. But the Bible shows us through the blessing that rested on the tribe of Levi that because of Levi's repentance, they were able to get back their original destiny. Levi shows us how much God rewards those who are willing to confront themselves with serious self-scrutiny and character correction. Levi is a sign of God's unfathomable mercy. If we just

M&+
Levi shows us how much God rewards those who are willing to confront themselves with serious self-scrutiny and character correction.

take one step, God will do the rest. Out of Levi came Moses, Aaron, Miriam, and the tribe of Levi.

Numbers 8:14-18 KJV

[14] Thus shalt thou separate the Levites from among the children of Israel: and the Levites shall be mine. [15] And after that shall the Levites go in to do the service of the tabernacle of the congregation: and thou shalt cleanse them, and offer them (for) an offering. [16] For they (are) wholly given unto me from among the children of Israel; instead of such as open every womb, [even instead of] the firstborn of all the children of Israel, have I taken them unto me. [17] For all the firstborn of the children of Israel (are) mine, (both) man and beast: on the day that I smote every firstborn in the land of Egypt I sanctified them for myself.

[18] And I have taken the Levites for all the firstborn of the children of Israel.

Because of Levi's willingness to repent, Levi is going to receive back the blessing of the firstborn so much so that the entire tribe of Levi is considered as the firstborn to God. Even though it may seem impossible because Judah already has the scepter and is the king, God has a way of still working out our destiny even though we may not know how it is going to happen. Only it was not just Levi, but the entire tribe. God so honors our repentance that He restores us and sets us on high. Levi had one of the greatest callings in all of Israel. God does not call perfect people, but people that are weak, vulnerable, broken, in touch with their personal pain, and willing to go through the correction process by the grace of God.

Judah

Levi should have received the right of being firstborn before Judah, but the status of being firstborn went to Judah because he took complete ownership for his sins and responsibility for others.

Judah begins with a very dysfunctional personality: he is critical and self-righteous. He blames his daughter-in-law Tamar for the deaths of his sons, when really he is already disqualified from destiny because he married a Canaanite. Both sons were slain by the Lord and he deceives Tamar by telling her to go mourn in her father's house and wait until his third son is fully grown. Then he will send for her to marry his son, although he has no intention of giving his third son to Tamar in marriage because he blames his sons' deaths on this woman. Judah is displaying despicable character. However, the moment that Tamar brings the signet ring and the staff of Judah, Judah immediately repents.

Genesis 38:25-26 KJV
[25] When she (Tamar) was brought forth, she sent to her father in law, saying, By the man, whose these are, am I with child: and she said, Discern, I pray thee, whose are these, the signet, and bracelets, and staff. [26] And Judah acknowledged them, and said, She hath been more righteous than I; because that I gave her not to Shelah my son. And he knew her again no more.

From that point on, Judah begins to change. Judah begins to take the initiative and begins to come into his destiny.

This tendency of bearing ownership, recognizing one's faults, and at once taking accountability goes into his tribe forever. It goes down the line and is even seen in David, so that when David is confronted by the prophet Nathan about his sin with Bathsheba, he is just like his ancestor Judah – he immediately takes ownership and corrects his character (2 Samuel 12:13).

Judah also displays tremendous leadership when he and his brothers must take Benjamin back to Egypt in order to receive more food from the governor of Egypt (Joseph, but unknown to them) in order for the family to survive the famine.

Genesis 43:8-9 KJV

[8] And Judah said unto Israel his father, Send the lad with me, and we will arise and go; that we may live, and not die, both we, and thou, and also our little ones. [9] I will be surety for him; of my hand shalt thou require him: if I bring him not unto thee, and set him before thee, then let me bear the blame for ever.

Judah immediately stands up to his father, and offers to vouch for Benjamin, should anything happen to him. When Joseph demands that Benjamin remain in Egypt, Judah takes initiative and offers to take his place rather than leave his younger brother in Egypt due to his incredible integrity and the character trait of taking responsibility.

Genesis 44:32-34 KJV

[32] For thy servant became surety for the lad unto my father, saying, If I bring him not unto thee, then I shall bear the blame to my father for ever. [33] Now therefore, I pray thee, let thy servant abide instead of the lad a bondman to my lord; and let the lad go up with his brethren. [34] For how shall I go up to my father, and the lad be not with me? lest peradventure I see the evil that shall come on my father.

After Judah speaks, immediately Joseph breaks and that is when everything is revealed to the 11 sons of Jacob as to Joseph's true identity.

Judah steps up to the plate and takes the initiative with great clarity and responsibility. Leadership requires momentous movement right at the time that the miracle is needed. Because Judah was willing to take the

*MC+
Leadership
requires
momentous
movement right at
the time that the
miracle is needed.*

responsibility and take the place so his brother would not suffer, the birthright went to Judah, and Scripture says the scepter will not depart from Judah.

Genesis 49:8-10 KJV
[8] Judah, thou art he whom thy brethren shall praise: thy hand shall be in the neck of thine enemies; thy father's children shall bow down before thee. [9] Judah is a lion's whelp: from the prey, my son, thou art gone up: he stooped down, he couched as a lion, and as an old lion; who shall rouse him up? [10] The sceptre shall not depart from Judah, nor a lawgiver from between his feet, until Shiloh come; and unto him shall the gathering of the people be.

Scripture shows us that the qualification for exaltation into destiny for those that really want leadership positions and destiny is that we must be willing to put our lives on the line. That is the reason why we have the birth order in Exodus 1:2. Reuben lost the right of being firstborn, then Simeon and Levi lost it because of their anger, and finally it went to Judah. As soon as Levi repented, he recovered.

Prayer

Dear Lord,

Teach me how to walk in the level of authority and dominion and greatness that you've called me to. Never let me lower the level of my thinking to my ego or to my selfish desires. Let me always think of others before I think of myself. In the name of Jesus, amen!

Reflection Questions

Please answer these questions truthfully and not from a fear-ridden orientation, self-imposed guilt, or a need to be approved.

1. How am I currently taking responsibility? Am I taking responsibility for anyone else besides myself and my family? Do I take responsibility for others in prayer, or when I see someone in need? Do I take responsibility when I hear gossip to fix the situation, when someone's reputation is being damaged, to speak the truth? Do I take responsibility when someone is in trouble to help remedy the situation, or do I run?

2. In what ways am I locked up in Mitsrayim? What has restricted my soul from reaching its highest potential and restricted my destiny from reaching its highest place? What steps can I take to reach my highest destiny?

CHAPTER TWO

The Selfishness Syndrome

-Elimelech, Mahlon, Chilion, Orpah-

Can you imagine being a princess, the daughter of a great and famous king, in one of the most elite kingdoms of the Middle East? This is the true story of a daughter of destiny. Ruth was the daughter of King Eglon of Moab but because of Ruth's love for the God of Israel, she forsook everything for the sake of chesed.

I've often been asked the question, "What is the greatest of all character traits?" Jesus told us in Matthew 22:36-40 that the greatest (weightiest) of all commandments are two. From these two commandments, we extract one character trait. It is the greatest of all. It cannot be compared to any other. It definitely has a rank. Paul said, "The greatest of these is charity" (1 Corinthians 13:13). The Hebrew equivalent to charity is chesed. When one seeks after chesed and finally encounters it, one will give everything up to embrace it.

Song of Solomon 8:7 KJV
Many waters cannot quench love, neither can the floods drown it: if a man would give all the substance of his house for love, it would utterly be contemned.

Matthew 13:44 KJV
Again, the kingdom of heaven is like unto treasure hid in a field; the which when a man hath found, he hideth, and for joy thereof goeth and selleth all that he hath, and buyeth that field.

When we see Ruth, we begin to understand what the love of God is all about. She was not a Torah scholar; in fact, she was raised in an environment of idolatry and the cruel practice of child sacrifice. She came from the land of Moab, which worshiped Chemosh. Chemosh worship demanded that children be sacrificed and burnt alive. In her DNA lay tendencies and dispositions prone to selfishness and stinginess. Her ancestors refused Israel passage to the Promised Land, even though they had ancient family ties to the Israelites through Lot and Abraham.

How could this princess daughter of King Eglon experience such a conversion? Her life teaches us how we can change our world through chesed. She shows us that chesed can actually reverse the curse in our lives through Christ, when love is operating through us.

Let's take a look at how this amazing story begins in the book of Ruth.

Ruth 1:1-9 KJV
[1] Now it came to pass in the days when the judges ruled, that there was a famine in the land. And a certain man of Bethlehemjudah went to sojourn in the country of Moab, he, and his wife, and his two sons. [2] And the name of the man was Elimelech, and the name of his wife Naomi, and the name of his two sons Mahlon and Chilion, Ephrathites of Bethlehemjudah. And they came into the country of Moab, and continued there. [3] And Elimelech Naomi's husband died; and she was left, and her two sons. [4] And they took them wives of the women of Moab; the name of the one was Orpah, and the name of the other Ruth: and they dwelled there about ten years. [5] And Mahlon and Chilion died also both of them; and the woman was left of her two sons and her husband. [6] Then she arose with her daughters in law, that she might return from the country of Moab: for she had heard in the country of Moab how that

the Lord had visited his people in giving them bread. [7] Wherefore she went forth out of the place where she was, and her two daughters in law with her; and they went on the way to return unto the land of Judah. [8] And Naomi said unto her two daughters in law, Go, return each to her mother's house: the Lord deal kindly with you, as ye have dealt with the dead, and with me. [9] The Lord grant you that ye may find rest, each of you in the house of her husband. Then she kissed them; and they lifted up their voice, and wept.

Ruth 1:16-18 KJV

[16] And Ruth said, Intreat me not to leave thee, or to return from following after thee: for whither thou goest, I will go; and where thou lodgest, I will lodge: thy people shall be my people, and thy God my God: [17] Where thou diest, will I die, and there will I be buried: the Lord do so to me, and more also, if ought but death part thee and me. [18] When (Naomi) saw that (Ruth) was stedfastly minded to go with her, then she left speaking unto her.

In Ruth 1, there are four names that teach us how we can become trapped in the selfishness syndrome. These four names were actually changed by the prophet Samuel, who authored the book of Ruth, to indicate the character traits that God uses and the character traits that God refuses. The intent of the prophet Samuel was to deliberate the reasons why three sons of Israel and one woman (Orpah) missed their moments with destiny. Through this unique literary device of using names that are obviously not the real names of these four individuals, we see descriptions of a sick spiritual condition that comes from the character virus known as the selfishness syndrome. We don't know what the real names of these four individuals were. Samuel changed their names because by renaming them, he is going to spotlight for us some very negative character traits. Let's take another look at Ruth 1:2, which states, "Now it came to pass in the days when the judges ruled, that there was a famine in the land. And a certain man of Bethlehemjudah went to sojourn in the country of Moab, he, and his wife, and his two sons."

Samuel is going to tell us the man's name in the next verse, but deliberately does not tell us his name in the first verse because Scripture is indicating that his character is so despicable that his name is not going to be mentioned in Torah. He is going to be referred to as "a certain man."

Therefore the Scripture has withdrawn an identity from him.

It is a deliberate attempt on Samuel's part to call him a certain man, when he was not just a certain man – he was a very important man. He was a judge in Israel and a very wealthy man. He was one of the wealthiest men in Bethlehem and his responsibility was to be a judge amongst the people. Scripture is withdrawing his identity from us in the first verse to let us know that he lost his identity as a man of God, and he lost his identity and his heritage in Israel through his selfish behavior. The scripture shows us that he went to sojourn in the country of Moab, or in Hebrew, "the fields of Moab."

Therefore we know that he headed to Moab because there were fields of harvest that had not yet been affected in Moab, even though the land of Israel was in a famine. So the question is, what was so wrong about fleeing to Moab during a famine? How could this possibly be wrong? Beloved, what we need to see is that the text is teaching us that this "certain man" was so subjected to the negative character trait of selfishness that he ended up in the land where stinginess and selfishness were a way of life. This man also failed to perceive the true perception of power, that we receive blessing for the benefit of someone else. This man did not understand why God had given him wealth, and he did not understand the concept of achrayut, or responsibility. Achrayut comes from the Hebrew word "acher" (Strong's Hebrew 312), which means "another." Achrayut means that "I am your responsibility and you are my responsibility," and it is one of the most important success secrets in the Bible. This man did not understand that the reason God had given him wealth was because God knew that there was going to be a famine, and this man was called to be a distributor of God's goods to his brethren and to all the people of Judah who were starving and did not have enough food.

People were dying from not having enough food to eat and this man, whose name was Elimelech (Ruth 1:2), had the means to alleviate their sufferings. But rather than sharing his goods, his riches, and his abundance with the people that were literally starving to death in a famine, he chose instead to hightail it to Moab to try to save his own life. But we should remember that Jesus said, "Whosoever saves his life is going to lose it. But whosoever loses his life for my sake is going to find it" (Matthew 16:25).

The Bible is going to compare this great man in Israel, a man who had studied the Torah and was a judge of his people, with a Moabitess who had no Torah learning whatsoever and came from an idolatrous society, but accepted the God of Israel during her conversion and became a person of tremendous character. And we are going to see again that there are character traits that God uses and character traits that God refuses.

In Ruth 1:2, we see that the name of Elimelech's wife was Naomi, and she was the only one whose original name was kept. The name Elimelech means "let kingship come to me," which says something about his personality. The names of Naomi's and Elimelech's two sons were Mahlon and Chilion. As soon as this family arrived in Moab, Elimelech died, and his two sons remained there for 10 more years. The first son's name, Mahlon, means "sickness" in Hebrew. There's no way that any Hebrew mother would give this name to her son. The prophet Samuel called him "sickness" because that was the fruit of his father's selfishness. And the name of the second son was Chilion, which means "extinction." The Midrash tells us that the sons had other names, but the prophetic names that the prophet Samuel gave these two are "sickness" and "extinction."

This shows us that when we choose a path of selfishness and do not consider our neighbor our responsibility, we are walking into a path of sickness and a path of extinction. The first son's name, Mahlon or "sickness," indicates that selfishness can lead not just to physical sickness, but also emotional sickness and mental sickness. Sometimes our emotions can become so self-centered that we can actually damage our destiny through these negative emotions. The next son's name is "Chilion" which comes from the Hebrew word "kalah" (Strong's Hebrew 3615) and means "extinction." This indicates that people who are stuck in their selfishness can actually choose a path that is going to keep them stuck and they are never going to get on to God's real plan for their life. They are going to miss it altogether. Their destiny is going to become extinct because of the negative character traits that they chose to have.

> *MC+*
> *When we choose a path of selfishness and do not consider our neighbor our responsibility, we are walking into a path of sickness and a path of extinction.*

The Bible says in Philippians 2:5 that it is very important that we "let this mind that was in Christ Jesus also be in us." The context in Philippians 2:4 also says, "Let every man not think on himself but also think on the things of others, preferring one another." We are being commanded to not only think about our own needs, but also about the needs of others. Our minds have to be trained to think about somebody else's needs before our own needs.

Do We Live with Human Love or Divine Love?

So we see that Elimelech, Mahlon, and Chilion died without fulfilling their destinies. The fourth person that we see in Ruth 1 is Orpah. Orpah is the sister of Ruth, and her name is taken from the Hebrew root "oreph" (Strong's Hebrew 6203), which means "back of the neck." Orpah's name means that she turned her back on Naomi. She did not look after Naomi's needs, but she superficially cried, and as soon as Naomi released her, she went right back to her own life. So we see Orpah is a prophetic prefiguring of the difference between those who love their neighbor with human love, and those who love their neighbor with divine love.

We can love our neighbor with human love, but human love will only take us so far. We can be really good people who are nice, sweet, bubbly, lovely, and kind to everyone, but we are still loving with human love. Human love will never take us to a place of dying to ourselves for another person. Human love will never prefer others if we will not get anything out of it. Human love will always have some kind of bargaining in it. Human love has an attitude that says, "I am giving you mercy and love, because in the long run I am going to get something out of it."

God's love says, "I am doing this purely out of love for you and I am not looking for anything in return." This is called gemilut hasadim, or acts of loving-kindness. We see this distinction between human love and divine love. Our love must go beyond human love. Scripture says in Ruth 1:9 that "(Ruth and Orpah) lifted up their voices and wept" when Naomi wanted to go back to Bethlehem after 10 years. Naomi did not want to take her daughters-in-law with her because they were Moabitesses and she knew life in Israel would be difficult for all of them. Ruth 1:14 continues and tells us that "they lifted up their

MC+

God's love says, "I am doing this purely out of love for you and I am not looking for anything in return."

voices and wept again: and Orpah kissed her mother-in-law; but Ruth clave unto her."

Orpah simply said goodbye; she turned her neck and did not feel that there was any responsibility involved because there were no more ties now that her husband, Naomi's son, had died. This is human love. Orpah represents the back of the neck, or love that is superficial. In contrast, Ruth's love is sacrificial. There is a major difference between superficial and sacrificial love.

Elimelech, Mahlon, Chilion, and Orpah were stuck in the selfishness syndrome. Now we will see what was so different about Ruth. First of all, we need to understand that the Boaz Blessing is actually a blessing that is going to reverse the curse. We will understand that the first blessing in the Boaz Blessing is that God is going to promise us life after loss. There are some of us who have gone through tremendous losses in our lives, but the Boaz Blessing is a promise that God is a God of restoration after the devastation that we have been through. God is the kind of God who is going to give us life after loss. It does not matter how much we have lost; we serve a God who is able to bring life after loss in our lives.

In Ruth 1, there is a compassion in the context that validates the years of tears of people that are living with loss. Ruth 1:5 states, "Mahlon and Chilion died; and the woman was left of her two sons and her husband." Naomi went through tremendous loss in a 10-year period. When her husband made the mistake of going to the land of Moab because he did not want to share his bread or his resources with anyone, he died soon thereafter. And the two sons died within a 10-year period. Naomi lost everything because all of the riches that her husband and sons took out of Bethlehem; they had taken all the money and did not leave anything behind in Bethlehem. They did not say, "We will leave this for our relatives. Let's leave 20,000 shekels of silver for our nephews and nieces; let's keep something for others in our family." No, they took everything they owned and moved to Moab, and as a result, all of their wealth diminished in Moab. Naomi had nothing left. And now Scripture says that Naomi is going to have to go back to Bethlehem to reclaim her family's property. She knows that when she gets back to Bethlehem that all the people who live in Bethlehem are going to say, "Look what happened to Naomi: she left as a very rich lady, but she's coming back with nothing. She doesn't even have her husband or her two sons, and she has no wealth because that family refused to share their abundance with any of us."

It was obvious that the hand of God had come against that family for the deadly decision of selfishness. Ruth 1:19 states, "So they two went until they came to Bethlehem.... All the city was moved about them, and they said, is this Naomi?" They could not believe it was Naomi because she looked so different. And Naomi said, "Do not call me Naomi, but call me Mara, for the Lord Almighty hath dealt very bitterly with me. I went out full and the Lord hath brought me home again empty." In other words, "I lost everything. There is nothing left for me. I lost my sons, my husband, my wealth, my reputation, our family name, everything. But I am coming back here to Bethlehem because I believe this is where I belong, because everything in Moab has been nothing but death for me and my family, so I am making a decision to return."

MC+
When we make a decision to return to God's best plan for our lives, we serve a God who can turn a mistake into a miracle.

When we make a decision to return to God's best plan for our lives, we serve a God who can turn a mistake into a miracle. There is a miracle of life after loss; if we will return, we can make the decision for destiny. So we see that there is a compassion in the context that validates the pain and the years of tears of living with loss. Scripture is going out of its way to show us Naomi's pain and that this is a tremendous ordeal that she is going through. The Bible is validating those who have gone through the terrible pain of living with loss. When Scripture goes out of its way to tell us the losses that human beings have suffered, there is a compassion in the context that says, "This is not your end. You don't have to end up like this." Naomi lost everything: sons, place, position, finance, wealth, everything. But we serve a God who is able to give us back double for our shame. We need to make a decision to return to God's best plan for our lives.

Prayer

Dear Lord,

I worship You and I give You thanks! Thank you for the many blessings in my life. Help me to live with a selfless love, and to always remember that I have been blessed to be a blessing. Help me to love others with divine love. In the mighty name of Jesus, amen!

Reflection Questions

1. Have you ever acted in a selfless way, for the benefit of someone else? How did your character develop through this act of selflessness? What was the outcome of the situation?

2. What are some of the blessings that the Lord has given to you (e.g., talents and abilities, finances, other resources)? How can you use these gifts from the Lord to bless others?

CHAPTER THREE

Chesed

The Diadem of Destiny
-Ruth-

As we continue in our exploration of the life of Ruth, we can see that when we make destiny decisions from our own free will, heaven takes over. Our steps are ordered of God. We begin to walk in the "hashgacha pratis" (divine providence) that guides and provides for every decision in our life.

The decision to go back to Israel for Naomi was one that required great character and resulted in monumental miracles. Naomi made the decision during the time of Passover that she was going to go back to Israel and not stay anymore in Moab. Isn't it something that she left Moab at the same time of the year that the children of Israel left Egypt, which demonstrates that God was breaking bondages? In Ruth 1:22, we see that Naomi and Ruth arrived in Bethlehem at the beginning of the barley harvest.

So Naomi returned to Israel, and brought Ruth the Moabitess with her, and they came to Bethlehem at the beginning of the barley harvest. We are going to understand how God can take 10 years of loss, 20 years of loss, or 50 years of loss, and if we have our heart right with God, then it doesn't take God a whole lot of time to start restoring back to us the years that the cankerworm has eaten and that the palmerworm has eaten (Joel 2:25). We will see that within 49 days, Ruth is going to receive back everything that the enemy has stolen out of her life. She's going to get double for her shame. During this 49-day period, God is going to start restoring back to Naomi everything that she's lost. Ruth and Boaz become married at the end of the 49 days on Pentecost, and about a year after that, God gives Ruth a son. The Bible tells us that the women of Bethlehem said, "A son is born to Naomi!" It was Ruth's son and not Naomi's son, but God gave that child to Naomi to replace the loss of her own sons. Scripture indicates that Naomi was able to nurse the child. This means that God provided a miracle by helping her body to produce milk when this was not her child, and she was past the age of childbearing.

Ruth 4:16 KJV
And Naomi took the child, and laid it in her bosom, and became nurse unto it.

When Ruth and Naomi first arrived in Israel, they had no idea about the kind of restoration they were about to receive. Do you think you know how good and merciful God is, and how God can restore? You have not seen anything yet. When we read the book of Ruth, we see that God gives us double for our shame.

Zechariah 9:12 KJV
Turn you to the strong hold, ye prisoners of hope: even to day do I declare that I will render double unto thee.

Isaiah 61:7 KJV
For your shame ye shall have double; and for confusion they shall rejoice in their portion: therefore in their land they shall possess the double: everlasting joy shall be unto them.

The book of Ruth shows us that no matter how devastating or how excruciating our losses are, God is able to give us life after loss and restore back to us one hundred-fold.

In the book of Job, we see that Job kept trying to figure out what he did to cause the judgment on his life, not understanding that he did not do one thing to cause the trials that came upon him. Job lived a life that was blameless and perfect before God. Sometimes, we indict ourselves because we do not understand the nature of suffering in our life: when God allows us to go through something, it's only because He is going to give us back double for our shame. In the process, He is testing our character.

Job 42:10,12 KJV
[10] And the Lord turned the captivity of Job, when he prayed for his friends: also the Lord gave Job twice as much as he had before. [12] So the Lord blessed the latter end of Job more than his beginning: for he had fourteen thousand sheep, and six thousand camels, and a thousand yoke of oxen, and a thousand she asses.

In the beginning of Ruth 1, the prophet Samuel (the author of the book of Ruth) writes Ruth's name simply as "Ruth." But starting in Ruth 1:23, once she enters the Holy Land, she is referred to as "Ruth the Moabitess" (Ruth 1:22, 2:2, 2:21, 5:5, 5:10). This is a very deliberate literary device used by the prophet Samuel: the word "Moabitess" is used five times when Ruth enters the Holy Land to demonstrate a very unusual prophetic prefiguring of the work of grace. Samuel goes out of his way to show that Ruth is the last one that we would ever expect to receive the honor of "Ima Shel Malchut" (mother of royalty), because her ancestors were among those who refused to give Israel passage into the Promised Land. The Bible emphatically states in Deuteronomy 23 and Nehemiah 13 that the Moabites could not be admitted into the congregation of the Lord, because they refused to allow Israel to pass through their lands into the Promised Land of Canaan, even though they were distant relatives through Lot and Abraham.

Deuteronomy 23:3 KJV
An Ammonite or Moabite shall not enter into the congregation of the Lord; even to their tenth generation

shall they not enter into the congregation of the LORD for ever.

Nehemiah 13:1 KJV
On that day they read in the book of Moses in the audience of the people; and therein was found written, that the Ammonite and the Moabite should not come into the congregation of God for ever.

Yet Ruth, a Moabitess, is the very one that God had chosen for destiny. This is why the prophet Samuel uses this unusual literacy device when she enters the Promised Land; this is part of his prophetic agenda. You may be the person that no one ever expected, or you may be one who feels that you are disqualified from destiny. But I wrote this book to tell you that God is able to break the bondages that have held you hostage from receiving all God has for you. Ruth's name is changed to Ruth the Moabitess because she is beginning to inherit destiny and the curse is going into reverse. We will see how the character trait of chesed completely changed the destiny of Ruth the Moabitess. We will see how Ruth

> *MC+*
> *God is able to break the bondages that have held you hostage from receiving all God has for you.*

the Moabitess became "Ima Shel Malchut," the mother of royalty, the mother of the Davidic dynasty, through the character trait of chesed. Just as possessing the character trait of chesed changed the destiny of Ruth, when we possess the character trait of chesed, everything around us will transform itself into the highest dimension of destiny that God has ordained for us.

Ruth is a reflection of the perfection of what chesed really is and what chesed really means. Chesed is the love of God in action. Chesed is not proud or boastful; it is not puffed up; it does not seek its own; it bears all things, hopes all things, and endures all things (see 1 Corinthians 13). It is the most important character trait for one to possess in the entire Bible. We are going to see what it means to lay one's life down for one's friend.

The name Ruth is taken from the Hebrew root "rea" (Strong's Hebrew 7453), which means friend. Ruth is a prophetic prefiguring of the scripture found in John 15:13.

John 15:13 KJV
Greater love hath no man than this, that a man lay down his life for his friends.

The love of God in action, chesed, was so exemplified in the life of Ruth that it reflects the perfect expression of the way we are to love one another. Can you imagine loving someone and not being bonded to them? Some of us have never experienced the security, fellowship, and acceptance of being bonded to another human being. Fear can hold us back from perfect love. As 1 John 4:18 says, "There is no fear in love; but perfect love casteth out fear: because fear hath torment. He that feareth is not made perfect in love."

> **MC+**
> *Fear prevents us from being bonded to another person because we are afraid of rejection.*

Fear prevents us from being bonded to another person because we are afraid of rejection, or we are afraid of being abandoned, or we have other insecurities that prevent us from the pleasure of being bonded to another human being. Bonding for a child begins with its mother, in the security of the mother holding the child, and the child receiving the pleasure of a mother's love. Bonding can also be expressed in the relationship between a husband and wife. The love between a husband and wife begins in the core of bonding. Genesis 2:24 says, "Therefore shall a man leave his father and his mother, and shall cleave unto his wife." Marital relationships demonstrate that we can be ourselves and still be fully loved. Without the element of bonding, love is incomplete.

> *MC+*
> *One of the most beautiful illustrations of bonding in love is taking responsibility for another person.*

One of the most beautiful illustrations of bonding in love is taking responsibility for another person. Naomi was helpless, elderly, abandoned, and in grief. Ruth was no longer Naomi's relative in the natural. Ruth's husband, Naomi's son, was dead, and there were no children, yet through her conversion to the God of Israel, Ruth felt a responsibility toward Naomi that required her to take care of Naomi, to bond with her, and to forsake everything to follow her into the Promised Land. Ruth possessed the character trait of "achrayut" or responsibility. She also forsook everything to help Naomi because she so immensely loved the God of Israel. Ruth's life shows us that if we love God, that love is expressed in how we love our neighbor.

Ruth 1:16-17 KJV
[16] And Ruth said, Intreat me not to leave thee, or to return from following after thee: for whither thou goest, I will go; and where thou lodgest, I will lodge: thy people

shall be my people, and thy God my God: [17] Where thou diest, will I die, and there will I be buried: the Lord do so to me, and more also, if ought but death part thee and me.

Beloved, we cannot truly love one another if we do not possess the character trait of achrayut, or responsibility. Complete love has the component of bonding and achrayut in it. The Bible teaches us to lay down our lives one for another, but to love one another in deed and truth (1 John 3:18).

Chesed is the crown of all character traits. The chesed that Ruth displayed to Naomi brought the curse into reverse in her life and became the means by which she became "Ima Shel Malchut," the mother of royalty, the mother of the Davidic dynasty.

In John 13:34, Jesus commanded that we love one another not with human love, but with divine love. Divine love will stretch us to become supernaturally sensitive through the love of God toward others.

MC+

Divine love will stretch us to become supernaturally sensitive through the love of God toward others.

Ruth insisted on staying with Naomi through the love of God.

When Ruth and Naomi arrived back in Israel, in the area of Bethlehem, it was the time of the barley harvest. God made special laws called the laws of "leket" for the poor during the barley harvest so that not only would the rich reap, but the poor would also enjoy harvest. When people were harvesting their crops, if they got too much in their hand and some fell to the ground, the gleaners could come behind and pick up everything that the harvesters dropped. The harvesters could not pick up any crop that fell to the ground because they believed that God allowed it to drop for the poor, so that the land could be raised up in its holiness before God.

Ruth arrived in Israel and she took initiative. She refused to allow Naomi to glean in the fields. Ruth bore the responsibility for Naomi and chose to take Naomi's place, rather than allow Naomi to be humiliated in the place where she was once a woman of prominence. Ruth worked the field for Naomi and was willing to come and go to the fields 10 times in one day so that Naomi would not bear the burden.

When Ruth was picking the harvest, she did not know that she was gleaning in Boaz's field, or that Boaz was going to take action because of all that she had done for Naomi. Boaz's heart was so moved for Ruth that he ordered his workers to keep dropping the leket on the ground for Ruth to pick up, and he allowed Ruth to get extra food to refresh herself. Someone of Boaz's stature never talked to a reaper of a lower status, but he talked to Ruth. By the time the wheat harvest came around several weeks later, Naomi passed her right to marry Boaz according to the laws of Israel on to Ruth (these are the laws of yibbum, described in Deuteronomy 25:5-10). Ruth married the richest man in all of Bethlehem, then had a child and eventually became the great-grandmother of King David and an ancestor of the Messiah, as a reward for her chesed! Beloved, let us make a decision to walk in the love of God and fulfill our destinies!

Prayer

Dear Lord,

I worship and adore You, and praise Your holy name! Give me the strength to make difficult decisions, and to base my decisions on the love of God. Help me to be sensitive to the needs of others, and to stretch to another dimension of love for my neighbor. Cause my character to be complete, that I would be pleasing to you in every way. In the name of Jesus, amen!

Reflection Questions

1. Do you show the love of God to others? Have you born a burden recently for a friend? Who are you taking responsibility for, besides yourself and your family? In what ways are you taking responsibility for them?

2. Do you have difficulty bonding with those you love? If so, why? Invite the Lord into the situation, and ask Him to bring healing, forgiveness, and anything else that might be needed.

CHAPTER FOUR

Coming into Perfection through Character Correction

-Joseph-

Beloved, have you ever looked at all the painful, disappointing, senseless events that have taken place in your life and wondered, "Why, Lord? What possible purpose could all this serve? What possible glory could You get from all the pain I've endured or all the tears I've cried?" I'm sure, beloved, that these are questions that we have all asked at some point in our lives. But has it ever occurred to you that God could be using those excruciating and painfully agonizing trials to move you toward possessing the promises and prophecies He has for you? We, as believers, know that there is no such thing as coincidence when it comes to God. The Bible tells us, "All things work together for our good" (Romans 8:28). And we will see this greatly demonstrated in the life of Joseph. But what we need to understand, dear one, is that as we journey on this road to the highest dimension of our destiny, there are certain aspects of our character that God desires to be developed and perfected. And this will not always be a walk in the park. Success comes with a price. But as we study the life of Joseph, for example, we will begin to see his secret of supernatural success. His success could never be achieved by human means. In a series of supernatural setups, God orchestrated and coordinated a destiny for Joseph that prophetically prefigures the heights of greatness we can experience through the grace of God.

The development of character is so important to the design of destiny in our lives that Scripture spotlights the lives and personal experiences of chosen individuals in the Bible to show us the character traits that God uses and the character traits that God refuses. The diadem of destiny in the lives of all of those who arrived at the gift of God-given greatness was challenged in the most vulnerable areas of their lives and emotions. This is why the Bible goes out of its way to give us a front row seat into the insight of their personal pain and emotional challenges. The Bible highlights individuals who, in their natural tendencies and dispositions, were tested with trials that affected their emotions, thought processes, and character. These kinds of tests were the greatest of all the challenges they ever experienced. For David, Ruth, Joseph, and virtually every chosen individual in the Bible, their test was not about the outward test! The tests of the moment that pressed and challenged them were tailor-made to prove and qualify them for the exalted diadem of destiny ordained for their lives. Like all of us, these heroes of the Bible had weaknesses in character that needed to be improved, polished, and perfected. The tests qualified them as recipients of legacy and leadership who changed nations and paved the path for generations to come.

The supernatural secret of the text teaches that painful places and tests are given to us for the purpose of coming into perfection through character correction. This means that these heroes of the Bible were not perfect, but they were willing to face the fight and struggle of negative emotions that could dominate their character traits. They sought out improvement through God and set an example of how we can overcome any character challenge through the grace of God.

Training in self-discernment and self-scrutiny can be one of the greatest gifts we can lavish upon ourselves by the grace of God. Throughout the Bible, it is the greatest secret of success. Taking responsibility and accountability releases mercy, grace, and double for our shame.

MC+

Taking responsibility and accountability releases mercy, grace, and double for our shame.

David said in Psalm 51:6, "You desire truth in the inward parts, and in the hidden part you shall cause me to know wisdom." Paul said, "I can do all things through Christ who strengthens me" (Philippians 4:13).

Nothing is impossible with God, beloved. If we make the decision for destiny, if we make the choice to appropriate the grace purchased on Calvary's cross, then we will be able to truly subdue our struggles and surrender our weaknesses.

If we look at Joseph, for example, we will see the secret of supernatural success. His success could never be achieved by human means. As believers, we know that there is no such thing as coincidence. Through a series of supernatural setups, God orchestrated and coordinated a destiny for Joseph that prophetically prefigures the heights of greatness we can experience through the grace of God.

In Genesis 37, the Bible does not present Joseph as a victim without hope. Joseph experienced astronomical success in Egypt and went from being a slave to being viceroy. His divine turnaround happened because Joseph corrected his character. His character was so corrected that he received a title given to him lavished by the rabbis. Joseph is always called "Yosef haTzadik," meaning Joseph the righteous.

Let us step into this remarkable journey of greatness through the book of Genesis.

Genesis 37:2-3 KJV
[2] These are the generations of Jacob. Joseph, being seventeen years old, was feeding the flock with his brethren; and the lad was with the sons of Bilhah, and with the sons of Zilpah, his father's wives: and Joseph brought unto his father their evil report. [3] Now Israel loved Joseph more than all his children, because he was the son of his old age: and he made him a coat of many colours.

In a Hebraic sense of scripture, the Bible is going to litigate some of the reasons why the excruciating events were allowed to happen to Joseph. These events are so important that Scripture dedicates Genesis 37-50 to detailing Joseph's suffering, struggles, and growth into greatness.

One of the ways that we develop acute hermeneutical skills is by discovering the intent of the author. What is the author's intent in Genesis 37-50? Is it just to record events so that we know that they happened? Is the Bible only a history book? Or does the author have a specific intent that is inerrantly inspired by God to leave a legacy for all generations?

Indeed, as this passage begins, the text begins to unfold that our beloved Joseph had some serious character issues that could have blocked him from the incredible destiny ordained by God for him.

In Genesis 37:2, the last line of the text teaches: "And Joseph brought unto his father their evil report." Can we put the brakes on here and back up? The scripture said,

"He brought unto his father an evil report" (a continual flow of evil speech or l'shon hara) against his brothers.

We can see in Scripture that evil speech or corrupt communication out of the mouth is one of the most negative character traits of a person's personality.

Ephesians 4:29-30 KJV
[29] Let no corrupt communication proceed out of your mouth, but that which is good to the use of edifying, that it may minister grace unto the hearers. [30] And grieve not the holy Spirit of God, whereby ye are sealed unto the day of redemption.

1 Peter 3:9 KJV
Not rendering evil for evil, or railing for railing: but contrariwise blessing; knowing that ye are thereunto called, that ye should inherit a blessing.

Romans 12:17-21 KJV
[17] Recompense to no man evil for evil. Provide things honest in the sight of all men. [18] If it be possible, as much as lieth in you, live peaceably with all men. [19] Dearly beloved, avenge not yourselves, but rather give place unto

wrath: for it is written, Vengeance is mine; I will repay, saith the Lord. [20] Therefore if thine enemy hunger, feed him; if he thirst, give him drink: for in so doing thou shalt heap coals of fire on his head. [21] Be not overcome of evil, but overcome evil with good.

Throughout the Bible in both the Hebrew Scriptures (Old Testament) and the Greek Scriptures (New Testament), the Bible strictly forbids the sin of gossip, slander, and other forms of derogatory speech (Leviticus 19:18).

Throughout the scriptures, the Bible teaches that there are lighter commandments and heavier commandments. Jesus condemned the Pharisees of Matthew 23 because they placed emphasis on the lighter things and put little or no emphasis on the weightier things.

Matthew 23:23 KJV
Woe unto you, scribes and Pharisees, hypocrites! for ye pay tithe of mint and anise and cummin, and have omitted the weightier matters of the law, judgment, mercy, and faith: these ought ye to have done, and not to leave the other undone.

As one who gives the perfect flawless interpretation of Torah leading all of Israel into the true paths that Moses intended, Jesus as man skillfully presented his rabbinic arguments to the rabbinic Pharisees who placed the wrong emphasis on the wrong things. Unfortunately, today we have a crisis of true character building in the church. Like the Pharisees of Matthew 23:23, we have placed our emphasis on the wrong things and failed to place our emphasis on the weightier matters of godly character and integrity.

MC+

What is gifted must always be sifted by character traits that qualify us and credential us for our calling.

In Genesis 37, the text teaches that Joseph's excellent business skills did not qualify or credential his calling. The text teaches that his "evil report" was based upon how incompetent his brethren were compared to his extraordinary exacting skills and charismatic ability that kept Jacob's flocks in a constant state of growth. However, what is gifted must always be sifted by character traits that qualify us and credential us for our calling.

In Genesis 37:2, the Bible says, "and the lad was with the sons of Bilhah and the sons of Zilpah." The English word translated as "lad" comes from the Hebrew word "naar" (Strong's Hebrew 5288). The word "naar" denotes biological immaturity and also emphasizes and could specifically relate to emotional immaturity. Although Joseph was an incredibly gifted business apprentice even at 17 years of age, he lacked the emotional maturity to get him to his destiny. The only way that Joseph, at age 17, could handle the deep rejection, unbelievably personal pain, and ruthless cruelty of being ostracized by his brothers was through using l'shon hara (evil speech) as a form of slight revenge.

Leviticus 19:18 KJV
Thou shalt not avenge, nor bear any grudge against the children of thy people, but thou shalt love thy neighbour as thyself: I am the Lord.

This mismanagement of his personal pain and rejection issues causes Scripture to show us that Joseph was not yet ready for the incredible place and position of power that he would have as ruler over Pharaoh's household and all of Egypt.

But Joseph did not stay stuck in his painful past. As soon as Joseph was sold into Egypt, impeccable integrity, kindness, trustworthiness, and wisdom began to navigate Joseph's life. Years later when Joseph became ruler in Egypt, there is no Biblical record that Joseph revealed to Jacob his father the evil that his brothers did to him by selling him into slavery. He does not have a session with his father like before when he was 17 and bring an "evil report" to Jacob, although now the evil is 1,000 times worse than before. Instead, Joseph never speaks a word to Jacob about why he is come down into Egypt.

The text teaches that there was an incredible correction of character and speech. There is not a trace of revenge, talebearing, l'shon hara, or even a grudge against his brothers.

Genesis 45:4-5 KJV
[4] And Joseph said unto his brethren, Come near to me, I pray you. And they came near. And he said, I am Joseph your brother, whom ye sold into Egypt. [5] Now therefore be not grieved, nor angry with yourselves, that ye sold me hither: for God did send me before you to preserve life.
Genesis 45:7-8 KJV

[7] And God sent me before you to preserve you a posterity in the earth, and to save your lives by a great deliverance. [8] So now it was not you that sent me hither, but God: and he hath made me a father to Pharaoh, and lord of all his house, and a ruler throughout all the land of Egypt.

Moses, as the author of Genesis, presents not just a narrative but a "prophetic purpose" in the text. The prophetic purpose of the author shows us a cataclysmic change in Joseph's speech and behavior (middot). The test of showing kindness where he was mistreated so unjustly, the test of not speaking evil against his brothers after they perpetrated heinous acts of cruelty against Joseph, qualified Joseph to be in his position of power.

Genesis 50:19-23 KJV
[19] And Joseph said unto them, Fear not: for am I in the place of God? [20] But as for you, ye thought evil against me; but God meant it unto good, to bring to pass, as it is this day, to save much people alive. [21] Now therefore fear ye not: I will nourish you, and your little ones. And he comforted them, and spake kindly unto them. [22] And Joseph dwelt in Egypt, he, and his father's house: and Joseph lived an hundred and ten years. [23] And Joseph

saw Ephraim's children of the third generation: the children also of Machir the son of Manasseh were brought up upon Joseph's knees.

The text teaches that even after Jacob goes to heaven, "Joseph haTzadik" only comforts, strengthens, and is concerned with the well-being of his brothers. Beloved, let us continue to seek after God's best plan for our lives and to always walk in forgiveness!

Prayer

Dear Lord,

I give you praise and glory! God, help me to always see other people and situations through Your perspective. Help me to always speak kindly about others. I decree and declare that I walk in continual forgiveness! In the name of Jesus, amen!

Reflection Questions

1. Have you ever been tempted to gossip, or to make negative comments about other people? Why do you think that you had, or that you still have, this tendency? What steps will you take to remedy this aspect of your character?

2. Spend some time seeking the Lord about the destiny that He has planned for your life. Are there any other areas of immaturity that might prevent you from achieving your destiny? How can you strengthen these aspects of your character?

CHAPTER FIVE

The Most Important Biblical Success Secret

Purity of Heart
-David-

Beloved, in this chapter we are going to see how David the king of Israel demonstrated character with the spirit of "tamim" (Strong's Hebrew 8549), or purity of heart, by handling his ongoing battles with Saul. As the secret of his success, David continually kept his heart pure in the sight of the Lord and did not allow any negative thoughts or emotions to reside in his soul.

Let's begin by looking at 2 Samuel 22 and 2 Samuel 23. These two chapters are part of the same prophetic unit, and can be viewed as David's eulogy and last words. 2 Samuel 22 is juxtaposed next to David's last words because Scripture is presenting David's greatest accomplishment in his life. The greatest accomplishment Scripture is praising is quite surprising. It was the purity of heart during the time of tests with Saul. 2 Samuel 22 is almost identical to Psalm 18, and describes the crowning culmination of David's work. We are going to see in Scripture that the behavior and character traits, or "middot" (from Strong's Hebrew 4060), that David portrayed during the time of his battle with Saul was the crowning culmination of everything he did in his career. 2 Samuel 22 is lengthy, but we will look at the verses from the chapter that streamline the author's intent and prophetic agenda, which is to demonstrate character traits that God uses and character traits that God refuses, with the reward of destiny in mind.

2 Samuel 22:18-25 KJV
[18] (The Lord) delivered me from my strong enemy, and from them that hated me: for they were too strong for me. [19] They prevented me in the day of my calamity: but the Lord was my stay. [20] He brought me forth also into a large place: he delivered me, because he delighted in me. [21] The Lord rewarded me according to my righteousness: according to the cleanness of my hands hath he recompensed me. [22] For I have kept the ways of the Lord, and have not wickedly departed from my God. [23] For all his judgments were before me: and as for his statutes, I did

not depart from them. [24] I was also upright before him, and have kept myself from mine iniquity. [25] Therefore the LORD hath recompensed me according to my righteousness; according to my cleanness in his eye sight.

The Bible shows us the way ("derech eretz" in Hebrew) that David behaved himself during the very painful period with Saul. This was the culminating crown of his greatest achievement. This was more important than anything else David did. It required more courage than conquering Goliath. It required more skill than establishing the city of Jerusalem. The character traits developed against all inward challenges became the apex of his achievement. David's greatest

> *MC+*
> *The character traits developed against all inward challenges became the apex of his achievement.*

accomplishment was conquering his own character traits, his own inward battle that he had on a daily basis with King Saul.

2 Samuel 22, which is Psalm 18, shows us that David struggled with his emotions and thoughts, because of this shocking emotional trauma with Saul, even after he became the anointed of God. The quest for "tamim" and

pleasing character traits became the sole desire of David's life. Scripture wants us to understand that this is the door that leads to destiny in our lives. It produces the proof that how we respond to individual character challenges is the most important criteria that determines our destinies. When we pass the test, we enter into God's best.

MC+
When we pass the test, we enter into God's best.

We also need to understand how important middot and tamim of character are to the heart of God. In fact, we can see that the Bible dedicates 59 chapters to documenting the details of David's behavior. We can see those details in 1 Samuel Chapters 16-31, which is 16 chapters, and the entire book of 2 Samuel Chapters 1-24, which is another 24 chapters. Then we have 1 Chronicles Chapters 11-29, which is 19 chapters. When we add them all together, we have 59 chapters that are concerned with tests that prove David has acquired the qualification for exaltation into destiny. We learn from Scripture that the quality of our character is the most important criteria to God. David is providing an example for us of how to handle the challenges and conflicts in our lives by tamim (purity of heart) and with pleasing character traits.

1 Samuel 18:6-11 KJV

[6] And it came to pass as they came, when David was returned from the slaughter of the Philistine, that the women came out of all cities of Israel, singing and dancing, to meet king Saul, with tabrets, with joy, and with instruments of musick. [7] And the women answered one another as they played, and said, Saul hath slain his thousands, and David his ten thousands. [8] And Saul was very wroth, and the saying displeased him; and he said, They have ascribed unto David ten thousands, and to me they have ascribed but thousands: and what can he have more but the kingdom? [9] And Saul eyed David from that day and forward. [10] And it came to pass on the morrow, that the evil spirit from God came upon Saul, and he prophesied in the midst of the house: and David played with his hand, as at other times: and there was a javelin in Saul's hand. [11] And Saul cast the javelin; for he said, I will smite David even to the wall with it. And David avoided out of his presence twice.

All throughout 1 Samuel 18, the author's intent is to show how Saul tried to sabotage David. These "traps" for David's soul were situations like Saul offering his daughter Merab in marriage to David, in exchange for David fighting against the Philistines. The marriage was designed as a strategic setup. Saul was actually hoping that David would be killed in battle. David was denied the opportunity to marry Merab and become King Saul's son-in-law. Saul was not integrous to his promise. David's great humility became the foundation for the formation of all the other character traits (1 Samuel 18:17-19). Scripture tells us that in all of these various trials with Saul, David continued to behave wisely and his character (middot) developed.

1 Samuel 18:14 KJV
And David behaved himself wisely in all his ways; and the Lord was with him.

Continuing in this context, the Bible shows us how Saul's jealousy toward David increased. He even took 3,000 men to try and kill David and his followers. The text teaches that even though David had the chance to kill Saul, he refused to have even a trace of the forbidden character trait of being vengeful. The following passage in 1 Samuel highlights the strength of David's character. It demonstrates that David battled and conquered the emotions that would fuel the fire for bearing a grudge. Bearing a grudge is prohibited by the Torah and New

Testament. In Hebrew, the root word for bearing a grudge is "natar" (Strong's Hebrew 5201). The Bible says, "Thou shalt not avenge, nor bear any grudge against the children of thy people, but thou shalt love thy neighbor as thyself: I am the Lord" (Leviticus 19:18).

Now, let's take a look at 1 Samuel 24:

1 Samuel 24:1-7 KJV
[1] And it came to pass, when Saul was returned from following the Philistines, that it was told him, saying, Behold, David is in the wilderness of Engedi. [2] Then Saul took three thousand chosen men out of all Israel, and went to seek David and his men upon the rocks of the wild goats. [3] And he came to the sheepcotes by the way, where was a cave; and Saul went in to cover his feet: and David and his men remained in the sides of the cave. [4] And the men of David said unto him, Behold the day of which the Lord said unto thee, Behold, I will deliver thine enemy into thine hand, that thou mayest do to him as it shall seem good unto thee. Then David arose, and cut off the skirt of Saul's robe privily. [5] And it came to pass afterward, that David's heart smote him, because he had cut off Saul's skirt. [6] And he said unto his men, The Lord forbid that I should

do this thing unto my master, the Lord's anointed, to stretch forth mine hand against him, seeing he is the anointed of the Lord. [7] So David stayed his servants with these words, and suffered them not to rise against Saul. But Saul rose up out of the cave, and went on his way.

Beloved, each one of us has a strong enemy, just like David had a strong enemy in Saul. The battle with Saul was a unique battle that would determine destiny in David's life. What happened to David will also happen to you. You will be given tests designed by heaven to determine your destiny. Take a moment to reflect upon your life. Is there any current test or tribulation that you are going through at this very moment? The secret is not to view this as some unbelievable tragedy that happened to you, even though it is quite normal to feel that way. The secret is that in reality this situation can be a gift if you understand that it is given to you as a test. This is a test like no other. This is a test for which the answers have already been given, and if you read the material (the Word of God), you will receive an A+. The examination might include the follow questions: Is your heart pure? Is there a tinge of revenge in your heart that causes you to speak evilly or negatively about the person that hurt you? When you think about the person that hurt you, does your stomach turn? Do you loathe the person that offended you? Be like David when he was faced with a strong enemy. Like David, some of the warfare that we encounter is actually a test. For David, the battle with Saul was the battle that would determine exaltation into his highest destiny, if he passed the test.

It was a test or an examination that would determine exaltation into his highest destiny if he passed it. The battle with Saul was a test based on David's character and emotional responses in a very dark, difficult, and painful place in David's life. These negative thoughts and emotions can arise because of the way that other people treat us, or because of spiritual attacks. David expressed how he felt when he was mistreated by his enemies, and even his close friend, in the book of Psalms.

> *MC+*
> *It was a test or an examination that would determine exaltation into his highest destiny if he passed it.*

Psalm 41:5-9 KJV

[5] Mine enemies speak evil of me, When shall he die, and his name perish? [6] And if he come to see me, he speaketh vanity: his heart gathereth iniquity to itself; when he goeth

abroad, he telleth it. [7] All that hate me whisper together against me: against me do they devise my hurt. [8] An evil disease, say they, cleaveth fast unto him: and now that he lieth he shall rise up no more. [9] Yea, mine own familiar friend, in whom I trusted, which did eat of my bread, hath lifted up his heel against me.

The battle with Saul was a test of character. David would be tested by whether or not he would take revenge, bear a grudge, or sin with his thoughts or words. Sometimes internal battles in our emotions aim to press us to sin with our thoughts or speech. This is what Psalm 39 teaches us about the battle not to sin with our tongues while the wicked are before us (see Psalm 39:1-3). The test with Saul was a proving ground for character traits. It was the place of testing and proving his "middot" (character).

Beloved, these things were written in God's Word not just so we know they happened. The Bible is much more than a history book. These things were written so that every generation may learn the pathways that lead us into the promises of God. Like David, you may be faced right now with a very grievous emotional battle that is pressing upon your emotions. You may feel dishonored, disrespected, and distraught over someone's behavior or over a similar situation. You may be facing the same challenges David had to face with Saul. Beloved, this may be a battle inside of you struggling with negative thoughts and emotions.

David is telling us that some of his enemies appeared to be loving or kind. But in reality, they only came to gather iniquity, to find fault, and to go abroad and tell it. Many of us have gone through the same kind of experiences that David went through. These kinds of experiences can cause us to have a feeling of despair or of being trapped in our souls, as we see in the following verses.

Psalm 35:12 KJV
They rewarded me evil for good to the spoiling of my soul.

Psalm 42:5a KJV
Why art thou cast down, O my soul? and why art thou disquieted in me?

Psalm 57:4 KJV
My soul is among lions: and I lie even among them that are set on fire, even the sons of men, whose teeth are spears and arrows, and their tongue a sharp sword.

Psalm 94:17 KJV

Unless the Lord had been my help, my soul had almost dwelt in silence.

So we can see that the most important battles that David faced were not physical ones, but were spiritual and emotional battles. When our souls start to feel downcast and spoiled, we don't process our pain properly. We see situations through the wrong set of lenses, and we blame people that shouldn't be blamed for our issues. Our discernment faculties are impaired, and our creative abilities are hindered.

> *MC+*
> *When our souls start to feel downcast and spoiled, we don't process our pain properly.*

It is important that we continually engage in self-scrutiny and see if these kinds of thoughts and perspectives are present in our souls. David understood the significance of self-scrutiny in maintaining a right relationship with the Lord and toward other people. Self-scrutiny is one of the most important components of character development. David continually practiced self-scrutiny, with the help of the Lord, as we see in the book of Psalms.

Psalm 139:23-24 KJV

[23] Search me, O God, and know my heart: try me, and know my thoughts: [24] And see if there be any wicked way in me, and lead me in the way everlasting.

Psalm 26:1-2 KJV
[1] Judge me, O Lord; for I have walked in mine integrity: I have trusted also in the Lord; therefore I shall not slide. [2] Examine me, O Lord, and prove me; try my reins and my heart.

The word "reins" comes from the Hebrew word "kilyah" (Strong's Hebrew 3629) which can also mean "kidneys." Just as our physical kidneys pull out toxins and purify our bodies, likewise our spiritual kidneys purify our thoughts and our motives, and bring the spiritual toxins out of our souls. If we have developed wrong attitudes, or if we're trying to cover up something and there's an issue in our lives that we don't want to confront, we need to say, "God, cleanse me, examine me, try my heart and try my reins, my kidneys." Like David, we must make sure that our hearts remain in a right attitude with the Lord and toward those who persecute us in any way.

David was a blameless individual, and he aimed to keep his soul without blemish in the sight of God with no bitterness, no resentment, no anger, no l'shon hara (gossip or evil speaking), and no retaliation whatsoever against Saul. This wasn't easy for David, because the Bible describes him as "ruddy," which means that he could get angry quickly and blood would rush to his face. The essence of David's battle with Saul was to trust God and to keep his soul pure. Once David conquered every motive in his soul, God rewarded him and he became king of Israel, as we see in the book of 2 Samuel.

2 Samuel 22:20-21 KJV
[20] He brought me forth also into a large place: he delivered me, because he delighted in me. [21] The Lord rewarded me according to my righteousness: according to the cleanness of my hands hath he recompensed me.

2 Samuel 22:25 KJV
Therefore the Lord hath recompensed me according to my righteousness; according to my cleanness in his eye sight.

Beloved, let us do everything we can to keep our souls pure in the sight of God, so that we can live in the fullness of our destinies, just like David!

Prayer

Dear Lord,

I give you honor and I give you glory! Transform my character, inside and out. Help me to understand the supernatural secrets of David's success. Help me to behave wisely in all of my ways, and to always behave with the love of God. In the precious name of Jesus, amen!

Reflection Questions

1. What are some of the situations or circumstances that cause you to become angry quickly? How can you handle these situations according to the Word of God?

2. Remember that we battle not against flesh and blood, but against spiritual principalities and powers. Keeping that in mind, who or what is the "strong enemy" in your life? What steps will you take to treat this adversary with grace and dignity?

CHAPTER SIX

The Gift of Self-Scrutiny

-David-

As we continue to learn lessons about the importance of character from the life of David, we will also see that aligning our character with the Word of God brings reward and blessing. We can see in 2 Samuel 22 (which is the same as Psalm 18) that King David was rewarded by God to possess his prophetic word in becoming king through passing tremendous tests and trials. Let us look at some of the verses that show us how King David was rewarded for his impeccable character during these excruciating tests.

2 Samuel 22:21-25 KJV
[21] The Lord rewarded me according to my righteousness: according to the cleanness of my hands hath he recompensed me. [22] For I have kept the ways of the Lord, and have not wickedly departed from my God. [23] For all his judgments were before me: and as for his statutes, I did not depart from them. [24] I was also upright before him,

and have kept myself from mine iniquity. [25] Therefore the LORD hath recompensed me according to my righteousness; according to my cleanness in his eye sight.

In these verses, King David is claiming that his ascendancy to the throne was because he did not depart from the ways of the Lord (2 Samuel 22:22), and that the Lord rewarded him according to his righteousness and according to the cleanness of his hand and eyesight (2 Samuel 22:21, 25). David knew in his heart that this incredible gift of God-given greatness in his ascendancy to the throne over Israel was due to God's loving-kindness in rewarding him for not sinning with his mouth or his thoughts, or taking revenge against Saul. Beloved, this ability did not come overnight. This kind of wisdom had been developing in David since he was a child. It came from handling lifelong suffering and rejection from his own brothers. David learned at an early age how to find favor with God. As a young boy, he took refuge in God's presence, in being alone with God. This "aloneness" came from years of rejection, which is highlighted by the prophet Samuel in 1 Samuel 16 when David was not called to the banquet.

1 Samuel 16:10-13 KJV

[10] Again, Jesse made seven of his sons to pass before Samuel. And Samuel said unto Jesse, The Lord hath not chosen these. [11] And Samuel said unto Jesse, Are here all thy children? And he said, There remaineth yet the youngest, and, behold, he keepeth the sheep. And Samuel said unto Jesse, Send and fetch him: for we will not sit down till he come hither. [12] And he sent, and brought him in. Now he was ruddy, and withal of a beautiful countenance, and goodly to look to. And the Lord said, Arise, anoint him: for this is he. [13] Then Samuel took the horn of oil, and anointed him in the midst of his brethren: and the Spirit of the Lord came upon David from that day forward. So Samuel rose up, and went to Ramah.

Let's take a closer look at 1 Samuel 16:11. "And Samuel said unto Jesse, Are here all they children? And he said, There remaineth yet the youngest, and behold, he keepeth the sheep. And Samuel said unto Jesse, Send and fetch him for we will not sit down till he cometh hither."

The word translated here as "youngest" is an unusual word in Hebrew, imbued with multiple meanings. It is not the usual word used for a youth; it is the word "qatan" (Strong's Hebrew 6997). The word qatan in Hebrew can mean youngest, but it can also mean least or most insignificant. In this case, the obvious conclusion is that it does not refer to birth order. We see in 1 Samuel 17:12 that Jesse had 8 sons, and we see in 1 Chronicles 2:15 that David was seventh in birth order. The Bible tells us in 1 Samuel 17:10 that Jesse made seven of his sons pass before Samuel. Logically speaking, if Jesse had 8 sons (1 Samuel 17:12 and 1 Chronicles 2:15) and David was the seventh-born son in birth order (1 Chronicles 2:15), then the obvious conclusion is that David is not the youngest in birth order. This means that the use of the word qatan in its multiple meanings in Hebrew indicates that David was the least or the less esteemed of all of his brethren. This helps us understand why Eliab his oldest brother answered him in such a cruel manner in 1 Samuel 17:28.

1 Samuel 17:28 KJV
And Eliab his eldest brother heard when he spoke unto the men; and Eliab's anger was kindled against David, and he said, Why camest thou down hither? and with whom hast thou left those few sheep in the wilderness? I know thy pride, and the naughtiness of thine heart; for thou art come down that thou mightest see the battle.

David's response to Eliab gives us insight about a life of rejection and constant belittling by his brothers. We read in 1 Samuel 17:29, "And David said, What have I now done? Is there not a cause?"

This also helps us understand Psalm 23. This is the psalm in which David gives accolades of praise to God on the day of his anointing. Psalm 23:5 says, "Thou preparest a table before me in the presence of mine enemies: thou anointest my head with oil; my cup runneth over." This is a direct connect to the day when David was anointed in front of his brothers by the prophet Samuel.

The Gift of Sekel: Behaving Oneself Wisely

The kind of experiences that David had during his early years caused him to develop a very unique character trait. It is the character trait of "sekel" (Strong's Hebrew 7922). Sekel is developed from the inward faculties being trained in self-scrutiny, self-examination, and truth. Let's look at several scriptures to explore this concept in further detail.

1 Samuel 18:5 KJV

And David went out whithersoever Saul sent him, and behaved himself wisely: and Saul set him over the men of war, and he was accepted in the sight of all the people, and also in the sight of Saul's servants.

1 Samuel 18:14 KJV

And David behaved himself wisely in all his ways; and the Lord was with him.

1 Samuel 18:15 KJV

Wherefore when Saul saw that (David) behaved himself very wisely, he was afraid of him.

1 Samuel 18:30 KJV

Then the princes of the Philistines went forth: and it came to pass, after they went forth, that David behaved himself more wisely than all the servants of Saul; so that his name was much set by.

In the verses above, we see the phrase "behaved himself wisely" mentioned four times. Whenever we see something recorded multiple times, we are looking at a pattern, which means that Scripture is trying to communicate something important to us. In this case, the author's intent is to communicate the supernatural secret of David's success which parallels with 2 Samuel 22 as we mentioned before.

The word "wisely" here is the word "sekel" in Hebrew. Sekel is one of the words in Hebrew that denotes wisdom. However, this word is not the exact same word as the Hebrew word "chokmah" (Strong's Hebrew 2451, 2452) which means "wisdom." The word sekel is a word that implies "to perceive something" or "to be perceptive." Sekel is the character trait of proper perception. And that proper perception becomes our protection when we are dealing with our enemies.

What is Scripture trying to show us in the book of 1 Samuel, verses 5, 14, 15, and 30? Well, first let's take a look at what Scripture is *not* showing us. Scripture is not communicating to us that David behaved himself wisely during his testing and trials because he was a smart or intelligent person. What Scripture is communicating to us in these verses is that David behaved himself more wisely in all his ways in his responses to the opposition that he was constantly receiving from Saul, because his ways were not only ways that pleased God, but they were the ways *of God*. Because David behaved in this manner, Saul became very afraid of him, not because of anything in the natural, but because David's personality and character traits became so much like those of God.

Beloved, Scripture is teaching us that the enemy pursuing us is going to become afraid of us because of our character. When our character becomes a character that reflects God's heart, the enemy will begin to fear us because he sees Jesus in us. Our character and the way we respond determine the level of how our enemy will respond to our situation. We can either allow our enemies to keep pursuing us, or we can put our enemies on the run through having a character that truly reflects God's heart.

> *MC+*
> *When our character becomes a character that reflects God's heart, the enemy will begin to fear us because he sees Jesus in us.*

Behaving oneself wisely in all one's ways in Hebrew is also called "derech eretz," which means that we are directed and perfected by observing God's commandments in all our ways, in the way we think, and in our personalities. David reveals this concept to us in the Psalms:

Psalm 23:3 KJV

He restoreth my soul: he leadeth me in the paths of righteousness for his name's sake.

Psalm 32:8 KJV

I will instruct thee and teach thee in the way which thou shalt go: I will guide thee with mine eye.

In other words, David is saying, "I'm walking in the path that is not just the path on the ground, but I am walking in paths that He is leading me on, in the way that I think and in the way that I process His Word for His name's sake."

Scripture also shows us that there are rewards connected with demonstrating sekel and behaving wisely.

2 Samuel 22:21 KJV

The Lord rewarded me according to my righteousness: according to the cleanness of my hands hath he recompensed me.

2 Samuel 22:25 KJV

Therefore the Lord hath recompensed me according to my righteousness; according to my cleanness in his eye sight.

We can see in these verses that David became king because he behaved himself wisely and overcame his internal battles with his enemies. David didn't become king because he was talented or because of his military skill. David became king because he was rewarded for his righteousness, according to the cleanness of his hands in God's eyesight as he overcame his internal battle.

David responded to Saul with humility. In fact, he responded with humility in all his actions. Why? Because humility became David's weapon of war. Humility became something that brought David into his promotion. Because David responded with humility, even though Saul continuously tried to set him up, he couldn't be set up because his character which had developed through trusting in God's Word overpowered his enemy.

Let's take a look at 1 Samuel 18 again to better understand the context of what was happening in the battle between David and Saul.

1 Samuel 18:6-11 KJV
[6] And it came to pass as they came, when David was returned from the slaughter of the Philistine, that the women came out of all cities of Israel, singing and dancing,

to meet king Saul, with tabrets, with joy, and with instruments of musick. [7] And the women answered one another as they played, and said, Saul hath slain his thousands, and David his ten thousands. [8] And Saul was very wroth, and the saying displeased him; and he said, They have ascribed unto David ten thousands, and to me they have ascribed but thousands: and what can he have more but the kingdom? [9] And Saul eyed David from that day and forward. [10] And it came to pass on the morrow, that the evil spirit from God came upon Saul, and he prophesied in the midst of the house: and David played with his hand, as at other times: and there was a javelin in Saul's hand. [11] And Saul cast the javelin; for he said, I will smite David even to the wall with it. And David avoided out of his presence twice.

We can see that Saul was "very wroth" in this passage, and that jealousy was rising rapidly. When Saul became very wroth, then an attitude of self-entitlement and jealousy came over him. We can then see that this attitude became an avenue for an evil spirit to enter. The Bible says, "And it came to pass on the morrow, that the evil spirit from God came upon Saul" (1 Samuel 18:10). Why is Scripture showing us that the evil spirit from God entered Saul? We can see from the above scripture in verse 9 that Saul is jealous, and now in verse 10 the evil spirit came upon him. Scripture is telling us that attitudes can open up doors for spirits. So we need to monitor our attitudes, beloved, because attitudes can either make us sensitive to the Spirit, or they can block the anointing in our lives. The wrong attitudes can be used as an avenue for an evil spirit to control our minds.

Again, 1 Samuel 18:9 says that "Saul eyed David." Let's look at the book of Mark for further explanation of what that phrase means.

Mark 7:21-22 KJV
[21] For from within, out of the heart of men, proceed evil thoughts, adulteries, fornications, murders, [22] Thefts, covetousness, wickedness, deceit, lasciviousness, an evil eye, blasphemy, pride, foolishness.

In these verses, Jesus says, "Out of the heart of men proceed wickedness, deceit, lasciviousness, and an evil eye." What is an evil eye? It is a work of the flesh. An evil eye does not involve superstition in which somebody gives somebody else an evil eye, and then bad things happen.

No, an evil eye reflects the condition of one's heart. And as Jesus says in Matthew 12:34, "Out of the abundance of the heart, the mouth speaketh."

Beloved, we must pay close attention to the words that we speak, both out of our mouths and inside our hearts and our thoughts. We can't say something cruel and unkind, and then say, "I didn't mean it." If something mean or gossipy came out of our mouths, then our hearts need to be cleansed. If it came out of our mouths, then we must admit that it's in our hearts. There are two ways of speaking: internally and vocally. Whether it was internal speech or verbal speech, it reflects what's in our hearts.

> *MC+*
> *We must pay close attention to the words that we speak, both out of our mouths and inside our hearts and our thoughts.*

So if we are making critical comments about someone, there's already a problem in our hearts. We can't deceive ourselves about it; it's already in there. Again, "out of the abundance of the heart, the mouth speaketh." We need to take ownership. If something critical came out of our mouths, we need to account for it and ask God, "Why did I speak that? What is in my heart? If I'm ungrateful or prideful, is there something going on inside of me? Why am I criticizing someone? Why am I so critical of other people's actions? Did I get puffed up? Did I get conceited overnight? What is in my heart?"

> **MC+**
> *We must continually examine our hearts and minds like David did, and get rid of anything in our inner being that does not line up with the Word of God, through the grace and mercy of God.*

Beloved, we must continually examine our hearts and minds like David did, and get rid of anything in our inner being that does not line up with the Word of God, through the grace and mercy of God. God desires for us to get to the next level. He's testing us and forming us through what we are going through. He is forming the clay during our trials and He is making us into a whole new vessel. A person who works on their character and relies on God's grace on a daily basis is going to be so rewarded by God. David is our example. God is not looking for perfection. He is looking for character correction. When we do that, we will fulfill our highest callings and destinies!

Prayer

Dear Lord,

I give You praise, I give You thanks, and I give you glory! Search my heart and my mind, and remove any wicked ways from within me. Help me to behave wisely in everything I do, and to always see others through the eyes of Your love. In the precious name of Jesus, amen!

Refection Questions

1. David behaved himself wisely in all his ways, which made his enemy, Saul, afraid of him, and eventually led him into triumph. Examine how you respond to your "enemy." Are you led by your emotions or are you led by humility?

2. We began to discuss in this chapter the meanings of Mark 7:21-22 and Matthew 12:34. How do these scriptures apply to your walk right now? Have you bridled your tongue or do you still need help mastering it? What ways can you improve both your internal and external speech?

3. Is there someone in your life that you are extremely critical of? If so, think of a situation where you were critical of that individual. Use the modified questions from the chapter to help you better understand that situation: "Why did I speak that? What was in my heart? Was there something going on inside of me at that time? Why am I criticizing this person and why am I so critical of this person's actions? What is in my heart?" Afterward, pray and ask the Holy Spirit to reveal to you how to handle this situation.

CHAPTER SEVEN

Downfalls to Destiny

Inconsistency in Character
-Saul-

Have you ever known someone that was very kind, selfless, considerate, and extremely humble? Then that very humble person overnight becomes a raging narcissist! You find yourself saying, "I can hardly believe it! He used to call me every day to see how I was doing, but now since he got that big promotion at work, he hardly speaks to me. Oh well, I guess he's too important to speak to someone like me now. I liked him better when he made less money."

What could have happened? What could have possibly taken place to cause such a dramatic and drastic change? Why does it seem like success can either make or break a person?

There are certain people who provide great examples of how to handle success, and not just any type of success, but success that could influence trends and cultures, and revolutionize thoughts and ideas. They also know how to handle success that has the potential to change destinies or the directions of entire nations. Such individuals are very rare jewels. Ruth and Esther, for example, were such individuals. They remained consistent in their character, never wavering, even after becoming extremely successful and highly influential. They always remained humble and used their platforms to help others. They knew that the blessings that they had received were not for the benefit of themselves, but for the benefit of others. These rare individuals and others like them, who continually worked on their character, understood the importance of humility, teach-ability, submissiveness to authority, and the wisdom of never allowing success to go to their heads.

On the contrary, there are others, who provide great examples of how NOT to handle success. Saul, unfortunately, is one of those individuals. There is nothing more disappointing than to see individuals who obtain success and were given the gift of great influence, only to use it for self-gratification and self-exaltation. They may have started off extremely humble, kind, sharing, and considerate of others, but once they received a taste of success, such as an unusually high promotion, an incredible position, an abundance of finances, or a great honor, all those exceptional character traits were abandoned or even worse, forgotten. These individuals lacked consistency in their character.

It takes great grace to be able to maintain altruistic character traits and still reach astronomical heights of influence and success. If not confronted on a daily basis, ego can change the destiny of a person headed for record-breaking greatness and cause it to spiral into a downfall. There is nothing more shocking and disappointing than to see that someone, who was at one time humble, selfless, and altruistic, has now drastically changed, because they allowed success to become their worst enemy.

MC+

It takes great grace to be able to maintain altruistic character traits and still reach astronomical heights of influence and success.

Unfortunately, Saul was an individual who was not found fit for the qualification of exaltation into the highest dimension of destiny. What do we mean when we say "the qualification for exaltation into the highest dimension of destiny"? We are seeing that God has prepared a destiny for every single one of us. There are certain criteria that Scripture requires, and certain tests that individuals went through that they had to pass. It is similar to the same way that when we are going for a job interview or we're ready for a promotion, we may have to take an aptitude test. Oftentimes when a person wants to go to a greater level of learning or to advance in their promotion and career, one must study and prepare for an aptitude test to see if one qualifies for what one is actually seeking. We have seen individuals in Scripture that God has raised up as role models for all ages, individuals who reached, by the grace of God, the highest dimension of destiny that was ordained for them.

We also see individuals that missed the mark and did not arrive at what God planned for them. How many of us would think that it would be a tragedy to know that God had prepared a great destiny for us, but somehow we missed our moment with destiny because of some attitude that we developed? That we missed it because of some character trait that held us back or some situation that we got stuck in that we couldn't remove ourselves from? Something that kept us going around the same mountain year after year, and somehow we were never able to put all the pieces of the puzzle together? We blamed the situation on everybody else, and we never took responsibility or ownership for it. This is exactly what Scripture has shown us about King Saul.

When we read the books written by the prophet Samuel, we see his prophetic agenda and his particular sense of style. The prophet Samuel is always comparing and showing us character traits that God uses and character traits that God refuses. Let's look at the person of Saul at the time when he began his mission.

1 Samuel 13:1 KJV
Saul reigned one year; and when he had reigned two years over Israel.

We know that chronologically Saul did not reign for two years. Everyone who understands Scripture knows that Saul reigned twenty years. But the intention of the prophet Samuel was to show us that only two years out of his twenty-year reign actually counted as part of Saul's destiny. Saul wasted the other 18 years because of an attitude that kept him from God's highest predestined purpose in his life. Saul was under the anointing and accomplishing the predestined purpose of God for only two years out of the 20 years of his reign. It was a premature death to a destiny. We see a ministry forfeited. We do not have time to waste on foolishness, and we do not have time to waste on a foolish attitude. We do not want to go through any time in our lives that there is a premature death to what God's called us to do.

We can see that the prophet Samuel is very specific in the way that he begins. He is preparing us for the reasons why Saul lost his destiny. He begins the text with "Saul reigned one year; and when he had reigned two years over Israel" (1 Samuel 13:1). So he has consolidated the fact that 18 years of Saul's ministry was seen as lost in the eyes of heaven. Saul never fully entered into the full heritage and the full predestined promise and purpose that God had for him.

Remember that there are character traits that God uses and character traits that God refuses. We see that God gave Saul an opportunity to heed the Lord many times in the book of 1 Samuel.

1 Samuel 10:8 KJV

(Samuel said to Saul) And thou shalt go down before me to Gilgal; and, behold, I will come down unto thee, to offer burnt offerings, and to sacrifice sacrifices of peace offerings: seven days shalt thou tarry, till I come to thee, and shew thee what thou shalt do.

But Saul did not fully listen to and obey the Lord through the words of the prophet Samuel, as we see in the following verses.

1 Samuel 13:8-14 KJV

[8] And (Saul) tarried seven days, according to the set time that Samuel had appointed: but Samuel came not to Gilgal; and the people were scattered from him. [9] And Saul said, Bring hither a burnt offering to me, and peace offerings. And he offered the burnt offering. [10] And it came to pass, that as soon as he had made an end of offering the burnt offering, behold, Samuel came; and Saul went out to meet him, that he might salute him. [11] And Samuel said, What hast thou done? And Saul said, Because I saw that the people were scattered from me, and that thou camest not within the days appointed, and that the Philistines gathered themselves together at Michmash; [12] Therefore

said I, The Philistines will come down now upon me to Gilgal, and I have not made supplication unto the Lord: I forced myself therefore, and offered a burnt offering. [13] And Samuel said to Saul, Thou hast done foolishly: thou hast not kept the commandment of the Lord thy God, which he commanded thee: for now would the Lord have established thy kingdom upon Israel for ever. [14] But now thy kingdom shall not continue: the Lord hath sought him a man after his own heart, and the Lord hath commanded him to be captain over his people, because thou hast not kept that which the Lord commanded thee.

We see in the passage of scripture above that Saul was supposed to wait seven days until the prophet Samuel came to Gilgal before offering a burnt offering and peace offerings to the Lord. But Saul became nervous as the time approached and Samuel still hadn't arrived, so he went ahead and offered the burnt offering and peace offerings. As soon as he was finished, Samuel arrived. Moreover, when Samuel asked Saul what he had done, Saul tried to justify his behavior. Then Samuel said to Saul, "You have acted foolishly. You haven't kept the commandment of the Lord. If you had, the Lord would have established your kingdom in Israel forever. But now your kingdom will not continue."

Saul lost his legacy because he missed God's perfect plan. And he missed it to such a degree that not one of Saul's descendants sat on a throne after him.

But do you know how good God is and how merciful God is? God does not want to see us lose our destiny. Oftentimes we make foolish decisions, but God gives us space and time to turn things around. He gives us situations to warn us and says, "Watch it, you're on shaking ground! Watch that attitude!" It's not His intention to take our destiny; He doesn't take anybody's destiny. We throw our own destinies away because of the choices that we make. Saul lost his determination and focus, but God gave him another chance. God will always give us the test that we fail a second time. We see that Saul received another chance to obey the Lord in 1 Samuel 15.

> *MC+*
> *God will always give us the test that we fail a second time.*

1 Samuel 15:1-3 KJV

[1] Samuel also said unto Saul, The Lord sent me to anoint thee to be king over his people, over Israel: now therefore

hearken thou unto the voice of the words of the Lord. [2] Thus saith the Lord of hosts, I remember that which Amalek did to Israel, how he laid wait for him in the way, when he came up from Egypt. [3] Now go and smite Amalek, and utterly destroy all that they have, and spare them not; but slay both man and woman, infant and suckling, ox and sheep, camel and ass.

But once again, we can see that Saul did not follow the commandment of the Lord.

1 Samuel 15:9 KJV
But Saul and the people spared Agag, and the best of the sheep, and of the oxen, and of the fatlings, and the lambs, and all that was good, and would not utterly destroy them: but every thing that was vile and refuse, that they destroyed utterly.

Let's look at what Saul said to Samuel when the prophet arrived:

1 Samuel 15:13 KJV
And Samuel came to Saul: and Saul said unto him, Blessed be thou of the Lord: I have performed the commandment of the Lord.

Saul was basically saying, "Look how good I am! Look what I have done! I have done this!" But he didn't perform the commandment of the Lord at all. What he actually did is disobey the commandment as he was told by the prophet Samuel. Saul was supposed to smite the Amalekites and leave none of them alive, smite everything they owned, leave nothing and not touch the spoil. But Saul took the spoil and he spared the best of everything of the Amalekites. And once again, Saul did not take ownership and tried to blame others for his actions.

1 Samuel 15:19-21 KJV
[19] (Samuel said to Saul), Wherefore then didst thou not obey the voice of the Lord, but didst fly upon the spoil, and didst evil in the sight of the Lord? [20] And Saul said unto Samuel, Yea, I have obeyed the voice of the Lord, and have gone the way which the Lord sent me, and have brought Agag the king of Amalek, and have utterly destroyed the Amalekites. [21] But the people took of the spoil, sheep and

oxen, the chief of the things which should have been utterly destroyed, to sacrifice unto the Lord thy God in Gilgal.

We also see in this passage of scripture that the prophet Samuel reminds Saul of the reason why God had originally chosen him to become king over Israel before he disobeyed.

1 Samuel 15:17 KJV
And Samuel said, When thou wast little in thine own sight, wast thou not made the head of the tribes of Israel, and the Lord anointed thee king over Israel?

Notice that character traits are reasons why God chooses us. Scripture highlights the fact that at one point Saul was "little in (his) own sight." Some of us forget and think the reason that God chose us was because of our giftedness. We think the reason that God chose us was because of our ability to sing so well, or our ability to be such a great sound technician or however we serve. We have a tendency to think that God has chosen us and selected us based on our adaptability and capability to perform a service well. But God doesn't choose us because of our gifts or talents. As a matter of fact, the text is teaching us that God chose Saul because of his former attitude of humility.

1 Samuel 10:20-24 KJV
[20] And when Saul had caused all the tribes of Israel to come near, the tribe of Benjamin was taken. [21] When he had caused the tribe of Benjamin to come near by their families, the family of Matri was taken, and Saul the son of Kish was taken: and when they sought him, he could not be found. [22] Therefore they enquired of the Lord further, if the man should yet come thither. And the Lord answered, Behold, he hath hid himself among the stuff. [23] And they ran and fetched him thence: and when he stood among the people, he was higher than any of the people from his shoulders upward. [24] And Samuel said to all the people, See ye him whom the Lord hath chosen, that there is none like him among all the people? And all the people shouted, and said, God save the king.

The prophet Samuel is showing us that when God chose Saul to be king and was to be presented unto all the tribes of Israel, Saul could not be found. Saul was chosen by God because of his character trait of humility: "And the Lord answered, Behold, he hath hid himself among the stuff.

And they ran and fetched him thence" (1 Samuel 10:22-23). Saul's humility was so great that he had hidden himself in a place where he could not be found or seen.

The text is also teaching us that it is one thing to be chosen and appointed for a position, but it is another thing to keep our position. We need to ask ourselves some questions about our character and our motives once we have been promoted. Are we holding on to virtue? How high do we esteem our character traits? Are we working on developing our character? Are we working on being humble? Are we working on being kind and considerate? Are we working on not being proud and puffed up? Are we working on becoming a servant and laying our lives down? Is there always a reason why behind every intention that we have? Do we have some hidden agenda that fuels us to do such an outstanding job in what we do?

MC+

It is one thing to be chosen and appointed for a position, but it is another thing to keep our position.

Scripture says, "For the Lord hath sought Him a man after His own heart" (1 Samuel 13:14) The Hebrew word "kavanot" means intentions or motives of the heart. Our motives and intentions of the heart are so important to the Lord. God wants us to always serve Him with kavanot, and not just go through the mechanics of ministry. We can be accomplishing all kinds of wonderful successes and still be living in a level lower than our highest destiny, because our intentions and motives caused us to live outside the realm of our greatest destiny.

When we are going through the mechanical motions of ministry, the intentions of our heart are not right and we are living at a lower level than the Lord intended us to live. Doing ministry in a mechanical way means that our motives are not right: we might be serving God to be recognized by others, or we just want to finish something so we can check it off our list and say, "I've already done what God called me to do. I have performed the commandment of the Lord." God wants us to listen to the Holy Spirit and then do our work through the Spirit. The Holy Spirit will give us the right intentions and He will give us sensitivity about how to perform our tasks with excellence. When we are not walking in the Holy Spirit, we are not walking in the power of our destinies. It doesn't

> *MC+*
> *God wants us to listen to the Holy Spirit and then do our work through the Spirit.*

matter how many things we do, or how many items we check off of our lists; if we haven't followed the leading of the Holy Spirit, we are living at a level lower than our highest destiny.

1 Samuel 15:22-23 KJV
[22] And Samuel said, Hath the Lord as great delight in burnt offerings and sacrifices, as in obeying the voice of the Lord? Behold, to obey is better than sacrifice, and to hearken than the fat of rams. [23] For rebellion is as the sin of witchcraft, and stubbornness is as iniquity and idolatry. Because thou hast rejected the word of the Lord, he hath also rejected thee from being king.

God doesn't want our sacrifice; he wants our obedience. God doesn't want our sacrifices of strife. God doesn't want us to keep thinking about how much we have done for God, which can make us prideful and make us take account of everything that we are doing rather than being humble and obeying the voice of the Lord. It is better to obey God in one little thing than to do 1,000 things in a sacrifice that He has not ordered us to do.

Samuel was grieved when Saul disobeyed instructions and did not serve the Lord with heartfelt intention. Samuel knew the destiny that the Lord had planned for Saul, and he grieved over the magnitude of this loss. Saul himself did not realize what he had lost, but Samuel saw the entire picture. Samuel saw the greatness of what Saul could have been, and how he lowered the level of his destiny because of the character traits that he chose to continue embracing. The Holy Spirit is grieved whenever we are disobedient and don't serve the Lord with heartfelt intentions. The Lord has incredible plans for all of us, but we have to follow His instructions with kavanot in order to achieve our destinies.

MC+
The Holy Spirit is grieved whenever we are disobedient and don't serve the Lord with heartfelt intentions.

Let's talk for a moment about presenting our bodies as a living sacrifice, and look at the book of Romans.

Romans 12:1 KJV
I beseech you therefore, brethren, by the mercies of God, that ye present your bodies a living sacrifice, holy, acceptable unto God, which is your reasonable service.

The word "reasonable" comes from the Greek word "logikos" (Strong's Greek 3050). When we see the phrase "reasonable service" in English, we might think that we are talking about service that makes sense, service which is right, or rightful service. We might translate that in our modern thinking as "Present your body as a living sacrifice, holy, acceptable unto God, which is your rightful service." But that's not what this word means. The Greek word "logikos" refers to the way we reason things out, the way we see things, the way we process information, and the way we should be serving God. Oftentimes we are in a place when our minds don't have fences or boundaries around them; we haven't trained ourselves not to be conformed to the world, but to be transformed by the renewing of our minds. The mindsets of the world and the actions of the world begin to cause us to render our service to God based on the standards of the world. But we should never let our service to God be based on the standards of the culture in which we live.

We need to continually monitor the thinking that goes on in our minds and not judge our service to God according to the standards of the world. The world is never going to understand our dedication and our service to God. This is why we must stay in the Word and be "transformed by the renewing of our minds, that we may prove what is the good, acceptable, and perfect will of God" (Romans 12:2).

MC+
We need to continually monitor the thinking that goes on in our minds and not judge our service to God according to the standards of the world.

According to the world's standards, Saul achieved a great deal of success. In 1 Samuel 14, we see Saul accomplishing one military success after another.

1 Samuel 14:47-48 KJV

[47] So Saul took the kingdom over Israel, and fought against all his enemies on every side, against Moab, and against the children of Ammon, and against Edom, and against the kings of Zobah, and against the Philistines: and whithersoever he turned himself, he vexed them. [48] And he gathered an host, and smote the Amalekites, and delivered Israel out of the hands of them that spoiled them.

But even with all of these military successes, Saul did not achieve his destiny and his legacy came to an end. Why? Because Saul did not have the character to sustain his success. Saul did not lose his legacy because David was more talented than he was. He didn't lose his legacy because somebody pushed him out of the way and took over. Saul lost his legacy because he didn't have greatness in the eyes of God.

What does it mean to be great according to the Word of God? Let's take a look at the concept of greatness in the lives of Abraham, Mordecai, and Job.

Genesis 12:1-2 KJV
[1] Now the Lord had said unto Abram, Get thee out of thy country, and from thy kindred, and from thy father's house, unto a land that I will shew thee: [2] And I will make of thee a great nation, and I will bless thee, and make thy name great; and thou shalt be a blessing.

Esther 10:3 KJV
For Mordecai the Jew was next unto king Ahasuerus, and great among the Jews, and accepted of the multitude of his brethren, seeking the wealth of his people, and speaking peace to all his seed.

Job 1:3b KJV
(Job) was the greatest of all the men of the east.

Job 29:11-17 KJV

[11] When the ear heard me, then it blessed me; and when the eye saw me, it gave witness to me: [12] Because I delivered the poor that cried, and the fatherless, and him that had none to help him. [13] The blessing of him that was ready to perish came upon me: and I caused the widow's heart to sing for joy. [14] I put on righteousness, and it clothed me: my judgment was as a robe and a diadem. [15] I was eyes to the blind, and feet was I to the lame. [16] I was a father to the poor: and the cause which I knew not I searched out. [17] And I brake the jaws of the wicked, and plucked the spoil out of his teeth.

In these passages, we can see that Scripture equates greatness with being a blessing to others. God can bless us mightily when He knows that we have the character to sustain the gifts that He wants to give us. Beloved, let us strengthen our characters and walk in true greatness so that we can walk into the fullness of our destinies!

Prayer

Dear Lord,

I give you praise and I give you glory! Thank you for all the gifts that You have given me, including the Word of God. Continue to help me strengthen my character and help me to obey You fully in every area of my life. I decree and declare that I will not fall short, and I will walk into the fullness of my destiny and complete Your plan for my life. In the mighty name of Jesus, amen!

Reflection Questions

1. Has there ever been a situation in your life in which you obeyed the Lord partially, but not completely? What was the outcome? Now that you have read this chapter, how would you have handled things differently?

2. Invite the Lord to examine your heart and mind, and reveal any areas of your character that need to be strengthened or changed. What are some practical steps that you can take to develop these areas of your character?

Books Authored by Dr. Michelle Corral

**For a Complete List of
CDs and Ministry Resources**

Contact:

Breath of the Spirit Prophetic Word Center
P.O. BOX 2676
Orange, CA 92669

Phone # (714) 694-1100

Youtube.com/DrMichelleCorral
Word Network on Mondays
@ 10:30 pm PST
www.breathofthespirit.org
www.drmichellecorral.com
facebook.com/Dr.Corral

59872010R00078

Made in the USA
Charleston, SC
18 August 2016